EMILY DICKINSON

WRITING AS A WOMAN

EMILY DICKINSON

WRITING AS A WOMAN

Mousumi Guha Banerjee

Delta Book World
New Delhi-110 002

First Published in 2017
ISBN 978-93-85719-02-8

Published by **Abhishek Goel** on behalf of

Delta Book World
G-4, Prahlad House
4832/24, Ansari Road
New Delhi - 110 002 (India)

Tel.: 011-4707 2321, 2324 5799
E-mail: deltabookworld@gmail.com
Website: www.kaveribooks.com

PRINTED IN INDIA

Dedicated

to

The Cause of Female Creativity

Acknowledgements

I wish to express my gratitude to those who have encouraged and helped me in various ways in the completion of this study. I am especially grateful to my supervisor, Professor Shanta Dutta, who has guided me throughout, by every possible means, and has painstakingly undertaken to go through all the chapters thereby minutely pointing out all the aberrations my writing betrayed. She gave her time and energy to me most generously to answer my questions, and I benefited greatly from her broad learning, critical acumen and imaginative insights. Her perceptive criticism and appreciation of my ideas were a constant source of encouragement and challenge to me. I deeply valued her ideas and suggestions. Her continued interest in my work has been of the greatest value to me; without the benefit of my encounter with her, this study would not have been possible in its present form.

I acknowledge too the courtesy and generous assistance of the staff members of the National Library, Kolkata, the British Council Library and the Library of the American Center, Kolkata. I am particularly indebted to all of them for their considerable support.

I sincerely thank my parents for constantly being there beside me whenever I was in need of anything. I also acknowledge the support of my husband, Anindya Banerjee, who has always been there in weal and woe. He has painstakingly checked the entire book and carefully read proofs of all the chapters. I have, from time to time, also shared my ideas with him and he has never failed to both encourage and enrich whatever I thought on the issues that have always interested me a lot.

I do not know whether a simple 'thanks giving' really would suffice for their patience, endurance and everything they have done for me, but I probably would not have been able to come out with this effort of mine without them beside me.

Mousumi Guha Banerjee

Preface

One of the most significant questions raised by feminist literary criticism is the degree to which women writers may be said to possess a voice of their own. The question stands double-fold when reduced to its essentials: is there such a thing as women's language and, if there is, what is the relationship between that language and the one which is employed by those who, in one way or the other, possess the social and cultural power to create the language against which, and within which, women may be said to distinguish and differentiate their own? This differential element has posed a problem in explicitly underlining women's discourse within the context of male-dominated systems of discourse. These are, at this developed point in feminist literary criticism, rather obvious questions; yet they are clearly related to my examination of the ways in which a woman intellectual in the Victorian period created and understood her own literary and intellectual performances, identifying the problem of the woman creator of literature.

Emily Dickinson, who is perhaps the most outstanding woman poet in the English language, certainly requires to be considered from the historical, subliminal, cultural and artistic standpoints of her femininity. The fundamental premise of feminist critical literature is that the essence of art and biography, and the correlation between them, is conditional upon the question of gender. That Dickinson is a poet is intrinsic to her creativity. By disintegrating her individuality into two mutually restraining constituents, 'woman' and 'poet', conventional critical thought has typified two characters instead of one. More instances of such a rupture of identity occur when her poetry exhibits traces of detachment from any significant evaluation as regards its relationship to the artist creating it. Feminist criticism endeavours to juxtapose these fragments together: 'woman' and 'poet'.

The present study therefore deals with the poetry of Emily Dickinson (1830-86), distinguishable and illustrious enough to represent her age, in order to show how the artist dealt with the problem of the woman writer in her works, at a time when the force of feminist movements reverberated throughout the society within which she created, and also how the woman intellectual emerged as an identifiable cultural figure. She, in her own unique ways, expressed and vented their scorn over the confinement of women to 'angelic' ignorance in the house. She wrote resiliently about the power of female art and female sexuality and the struggles of intelligent women for cultural autonomy.

The chapters of this book attempt to explore these diverse 'tides of life' that a woman poet experiences or, in other words, that Dickinson as poets might have experienced, since she belonged to an age that was so constraining as not to give her a due literary place. Dickinson tried to use the problematic nature of woman as a speaking subject in an attempt to explore and protest against women's roles both in her poems and in the society, but since the surface of her poetry – diction, subject matter and tone – did not contradict what Victorian women were expected to say, the shifts in point of view and revisions of old stories generally went unobserved and unappreciated. She expressed her deep concern over the duality in the roles of a woman which she is required to take on at her level of domestication alongside her intellectual creativity.

Contents

Introduction

'We perish – tho' We reign –': A Patriarchal Mirror and a Female Reflection

The nineteenth-century 'woman question' encompassed diverse avenues of understanding on women and their vocation, their right to enfranchisement, issues of single as well as fallen women and the flagrant circumscription of the dogma of 'separate spheres' that were supposed to be distinctly shared between the idea of the male and that of the female, the last being the most predominant conviction of the day. What becomes noticeable is a remarkable disappointment concerning the status of women in the works of several women poets of the time. Moreover, it was an immense responsibility on the learned women to examine the reason of female accomplishments being so exceptionally disparaged. In keeping with this tendency of thought, the ensuing literary critical discourses transmitted a considerable amount of parochial view to influence twentieth-century notions about nineteenth-century women's writing, which have often repudiated such literature as being too maudlin, too confined in their profundity and sagacity and too passé to communicate to a twentieth-century intelligentsia significantly. In one of her most refined of initial feminist interpretations entitled 'The Indefinite Disclosed: Christina Rossetti and Emily Dickinson', Cora Kaplan examines how Emily Dickinson, along with Christina Rossetti, deploys illusion as a mode of analyzing palpable female subliminal conditions. She asserts that we should be cognizant about the manner in which these 'texts speak to and about psychic phenomena in ways that are unique in women's writing of the period.'[1] This argument engenders a great hindrance for late twentieth-century critics of women's poetry of the previous century due to the fact that the endeavour of these poets towards achieving self-definition may appear to correspond unequivocally to the present-day concerns with commensurate possibilities for men and women in all domains of experience. There have certainly been ample perplexing difficulties that consider that poetry by nineteenth-century women gives a foretaste of the cardinal views of the Woman's Liberation Movement, as it evolves during the 1970s both in America and in England. The most complicated problem pertains to the propagation of the belief that there was a convention of writings by women that were supposed to be identified as entirely non-partisan to the extensive literary canon. But such a separatist approach might be perilous. Margaret Reynolds forewarns feminist critics against corroborating the proposition of a 'separate sphere' for women's literature, due to the fact that such an ethic may have its base on the principles that certified that in the nineteenth-century women were innocuously assigned a secluded and familial domain and are hence detached from a significant evaluation as creative artists. As a result, Reynolds asserts, a 'dangerous feminist folk-poetics is ... created – dangerous because it is, in fact, not more than a restatement of the classic values relating to women and poetry.'[2] She encapsulates the cardinal obstacles of this perspective:

> Feminist folk-poetics privileges women's experience, especially identifying an oppression common to all women (not allowing scope for their cultural, historical, and ethnic differences); it values the experience of the "self" (unproblematised in all but its contingent relation to patriarchy); it traces a "female" tradition (without any consciousness of the possible interference of a wish fulfilment) inherited from our mothers (qualified to endow by simple biology) which is usually an oral tradition (and consequently without trace) and often a mysterious one, related to a spiritual and moral sphere (which returns women's poetry to its conventional place).[3]

Hence, feminist criticism requires to be circumspect about echoing some of the most defacing suppositions against the essence of womanhood that have been implanted firmly in the ideologies of the Western ways of life as well as have contributed considerably to relegate the creative accomplishments of women to the periphery of all critical attention.

A few of these arguments have been aimed at one of the most outstanding works of feminist criticism during the late 1970s. In her critique against the oppositional humanist beliefs apprising the writings of several Anglo-American feminist critics, Toril Moi observes that Gilbert and Gubar's *The Madwoman in the Attic* (1979) offers an injudicious 'belief in the true female authorial voice as the essence of all texts written by women.' Moi argues that this conviction precariously 'masks the problems raised by their theory of patriarchal ideology' because '[f]or them ... ideology becomes a monolithic unified totality with no contradictions; against this a miraculously intact "femaleness" may pit its strength.'[4] Though it may so appear that Moi is in a way amplifying her opinion, her remarks are undeniably precise and unequivocal from a particular standpoint since there is certainly a formidable propensity in Gilbert and Gubar's evocative thesis to accentuate the ideology of self-affirmation with seldom any consideration for examining the way in which the poetic identity that finds expression in such a telling account accomplishes its aspirations due to the attributes peculiar to its standing.

In the United States, the most striking woman's utterance can be inimitably identified with that of Emily Dickinson, a poet who took up subjectivity as her theme and seclusion as an inseparable part of her existence. Despite the condensed, elliptical and contemplative features of both her poetry and of her letters, Dickinson studied and flamboyantly appreciated the teeming and diversely intrigued Victorian novels of Charlotte Bronte, Emily Brontë and George Eliot, who, in their turn, adopted the principle of self-assistance in order to typify the ideal of female creative individualism. Dickinson's poetic characters do not only embody female subjectivity, but she also presents the dilemma of the artist as an ontological enigma. She undertakes the enterprise of illustrating the state of subjectivity itself. In the following lines, she depicts a confrontation with the dead that is almost a transposition from the mundane to the transcendental:

I never hear that one is dead
Without the chance of Life
Afresh annihilating me
That mightiest Belief,

Too mighty for the Daily mind
That tilling its abyss,
Had Madness, had it once or twice
The yawning Consciousness[5]

The nineteenth-century creative minds did admit their dual paradigm of thought and belief. In spite of the fact that the age had comprehensively investigated the innate scope of the subliminal state of the mind, it was plagued by the underlying existence of class in the society. Duality was its prime characteristic. Considering the fundamental traits of the age, a woman poet had to assume a two-fold role, when she would attempt to identify herself within the poetic line of descent. Her predicament may be conceived as an imitation, rather contradictorily, of the truth that the contemporary society understood writing poetry as a woman's task, in spite of the fact that men were presumed to do it. Lucid and natural poetic themes were associated by nineteenth-century critics with unfeigned, truthful and unconstrained revelation of emotions – the ingenuous instinct that is still presumed by the critics to be the peculiar trait of women. Emily Dickinson's poetry betrays the incompatibility in the dual role of the woman poet more as an indispensable thematic strain than as a hindrance to eliminate. Dickinson perused the poetry of her literary grand mother Elizabeth, Barrett Browning with ardent consideration and probably she knew how to transcend such work. Dickinson prefers to locate her subjects within the sepulchre or without, and they distinctively correspond to flowers, children, inconsequentiality, vulnerability and taciturnity. But, in spite of such seemingly passive traits, they either tacitly or paradoxically claim their authority in their dissent against the conventional patriarchal ascendancy and the strain between the contradictory approaches is crucial both to the signification of the poems as well as to their structure – the inconsequentiality and the seeming puerility of the poems in association with their paroxysmal vehemence. Moreover, Dickinson superseded her British contemporaries in looking into the plausibility of either an unequivocal correspondence or a complete uniformity between the subject and the object. Her treatment of the subject-object relations indicates that the consequence was going to be an unnerving impasse which perhaps implies the reason why the other women writers, being more acquiescent to accepted forms, did not discard the fundamental pith of inconsistency that the question of gender gives birth to in poetry.

The emergence of a female poetic tradition does not necessarily hold criticisms that deal with the relationship between women poets and a male tradition of poetry untenable. It is so conceived that Elizabeth Barrett Browning, having no sufficient and continuing female tradition of poetry behind her, adhered to such a convention that is unambiguously determinable by and even identifiable with a male poetic authority that enabled her to bring upon herself a poetic prerogative. But this dialectic does seem to hold no sway because it can effortlessly be traced in poems of demurral throughout the nineteenth century particularly in those of Letitia Landon writing during the early part of the century and Amy Levy during the later part of the century. In Landon's case, a blatant sexual politics informs the conventions and practices that encumber women. Later in the century, one comes across more unrelenting utterances of disapproval in the works of Augusta Webster and Mathilde Blind. The poems by Landon and Levy are as engaging for their incongruities as for their indistinguishable subject matter. Landon conceives of marriage to be a culminating point of time that demands an involvement of self-immolation and oppression. Levy sees such a finality as reinforcing a patriarchal notion, since men advantage from profligacy and the delimiting intimidations of heterosexual partnership persist.

Hence, it is evident from the works of these women writers that there was created a women's tradition constructed on the basis of a complete and direct impugnment against subjugation. The presence of such a strong disapproval of a tradition of male hegemony often amounted to an obvious demonstration that can extricate the essence of an explicit diatribe about women's oppression, whereby the poem remains unsalvaged. All poems, in this way, unanimously and profusely voice the condition of women as they are situated in a particular point of time in the social and literary history of patriarchy. Thus, the content and language of such poems become problematically centralized on one particular idea.

The creation of a women's tradition confronts an identical impediment when a quintessential female domain of experience is taken into consideration, since it would imply the difference between two spheres of experience, male and female, which would result in a literary confinement of women's art to an entirely separate style or approach of writing. This may prove to be perilous and hence such art, though attempted by several women poets and critics of the nineteenth century who tried to achieve for women an unscathed position in art and literature, requires to be cautious since feminine sensibilities and the different modes of experience are conceived as being wholly discrepant from the domain of male thought, perception and sphere of existence.

The gender-based identification of poets as specifically 'women' is not beyond the hindrance of a group of women writers being considered as commensurate with a single male poet. Though the establishment of a distinctive feminine tradition is more often than not prone to be beset with such a pitfall, the dialectic of a familiar theme of subjection becomes clearly manifest. Most significantly, what can be traced from the works of women poets and critics of the time are the social predicaments of women, the adversities they experienced as writers and the manner in which these obstacles were overwhelmed. It is certainly obvious that through the writings of these authors is revealed a defiance against canonical male literature that so blatantly demonstrated the gender bias which, in its turn, actually facilitated the marginalization of literature by women.

The nineteenth century saw its inception in the conclusion of the French Revolution in Europe, sustained through the Napoleonic wars and terminates with a crucial imperial encounter, the second Anglo-Boer War. Quite evidently, the era begins with a type of poetry in colloquy with the most conspicuous conviction concerning gender where Edmund Burke[6] conceives of femininity as essentially pertaining to the injudicious and non-intellectual. Hence, femininity signified the sensitive attributes of the elegant that are substantially defined more by the supine female figure and less by artistic transcendence. The thematics of the New Woman evolved as a symbol marking the culmination of the century rather than an actuality. The concept went a long way in formulating a systematized feminist politics that manifested in most elaborate modes through the efforts of the suffragists. The New Woman turned out to be their precursor being enlightened with higher education and claiming for equality in private spheres.

Women's poetry has since then encountered several onslaughts of conventional and conformist standards of thought and practice by way of giving precedence to the concealed and personal experience over language, that was deployed only as a supplementing device. In fact, nineteenth-century poems of the British poets were thought to reflect virtuous and irreproachable qualities much in consonance with a kind of propriety and rectitude Victorian women were supposed to observe in their social behaviour, apart from providing a sentimental spur to men in the midst of their multiple engagements of life. Such a status might have prompted women to write poetry, but the distinctive features of women including qualities like, docility, acquiescence and quietude, tend to impede such creative writing. The doubt lies in the fact that women themselves conventionally being objects of art, there remains seldom any reason why they should create. 'For a woman artist is', maintain Gilbert and Gubar, 'after all, a woman – that is her "problem" – and if she denies her own gender she inevitably confronts an identity crisis as severe as the anxiety of authorship she is trying to surmount.'[7] They also summarize worthily the 'anxiety of authorship' felt by Dickinson by describing their experiences in the following manner:

> Emily Dickinson declares in one breath that she "had been hungry, all the Years", and in another opts for "Sumptuous Destitution" .... In addition, many of ... [the] literary women become in one way or another agoraphobic. Trained to reticence, they fear the vertiginous openness of the literary marketplace and rationalize with Emily Dickinson that "publication – is the Auction / Of the Mind of Man" or worse, punningly confess that "Creation seemed a mighty Crack / To make me visible."[8]

Gilbert and Gubar cite from an entry in Margaret Fuller's journal in order to enunciate this problem of the woman writer:

> For all the tides of life that flow within me, I am dumb and ineffectual, when it comes to casting my thought into a form. No old one suits me. If I could invent one, it seems to me the pleasure of creation would make it possible for me to write ... I love best to be woman; but womanhood is at present too straitly-bounded to give me scope. At hours, I live truly as a woman; at others, I should stifle; as, on the other hand, I should palsy, when I play the artist.[9]

The following chapters of this study would attempt to explore these diverse 'tides of life' that a woman poet experiences or, in other words, that Dickinson as a poet, belonging to an Age that was so constraining as not to give them their due literary place, might have experienced. She almost presumptuously, though often covertly, questioned the traditional ideals of femininity and gave expression to her creative anxiety either through a poetic representation of her self and subjectivity (Chapter 1), or through her poems on love (Chapter 2), or through those of nature (Chapter 3), or through her belief in religion (Chapter 4), or through her concept of death (Chapter 5). More than carving out a niché for herself, she has certainly been able to create a distinctive literary style of her own, that is no less unique, enduring and self-sufficient in the 'literary marketplace' than that of the commonly accepted forms of canonical literature, so much as to stay in the mind of posterity and to thrive for ages to come.

References

1. Cora Kaplan, 'The Indefinite Disclosed: Christina Rossetti and Emily Dickinson ', in ed. Mary Jacobus, *Women Writing and Writing about Women* (London: Croom Helm in association with Oxford University Women's Studies Committee, 1979), pp. 61-2.
2. Margaret Reynolds, 'Critical Introduction' to Elizabeth Barrett Browning's *Aurora Leigh* (Athens: Ohio University Press, 1992), p. 10.
3. Ibid., p. 10.
4. Toril Moi, *Sexual/Textual Politics: Feminist Literary Theory* (London: Routledge, 1985), p. 63.
5. Emily Dickinson, Poem 1323. All Emily-Dickinson Poems from 495 to 775 are taken from the following e-Source: *http://archive.csustan.edu/english/reuben/pal/chap4/dickinson.html* (Thomas H. Johnson ed. *Complete Poems* [Boston: Little, Brown & Co., 1960], as a part of PAL: Perspectives in American Literature – A Research and Reference Guide, An Ongoing Online Project, Paul P. Reuben [copyright])
6. Edmund Burke, *A Philosophical Inquiry into the Origin of Our Ideas of the Sublime and Beautiful,* New York: Bartleby.com, 2001. Source: *www.bartleby.com/24/2*
7. Sandra M. Gibert and Susan Gubar, *The Madwoman in the Attic: The Women Writers and the Nineteenth Century,* (New Haven and Roadon: Yale University Press, 1979), p.66. Quoted in Bell Gale Chevigny. *The Woman and the Myth: Margaret Fuller's Life and Writings* (Boston: Northeastern University Press, 1994), p.63.
8. Gibert and Gubar, *The Madwoman in the Attic,* p. 58.
9. Ibid., p. 71.

1

The Chiefest Apprehension/ Upon My Thronging Mind:

The Woman Author's Anxiety of Self, Subjectivity and Creativity

> (… England has had many learned women, not merely readers but writers of the learned languages, in Elizabeth's time and afterwards – women of deeper acquirements than are common now in the greater diffusion of letters; and yet where were the poetesses? The divine breath … why did it never pass, even in the lyrical form, over the lips of a woman? How strange! And can we deny that it was so?) I look everywhere for grandmothers and see none. It is not in the filial spirit I am deficient, I do assure you – witness my reverent love of the grandfathers![1]

How to position Emily Dickinson, in a literary tradition, is the argument that constitutes the cardinal concern of the present chapter. The recognition and acknowledgement of more women poets and particularly the creation of a Romantic feminine tradition with significant representatives like Felicia Hemans and Letitia Landon, has given birth to a literary domicile for the Victorian women poets, an intellectual abode that was not made available to earlier critics. Consequentially, they positioned the women poets in relation to a male poetic tradition, or in affiliation with the female novelists of the nineteenth century. In order to ensure the impeccability of these judgements, critics also attempt to examine and decipher the characteristic features of such a literary tradition. Sandra Gilbert and Susan Gubar apply and reconsider the Freudian model of poetic practice propounded by Harold Bloom in his book, *The Anxiety of Influence.*[2] Bloom contemplates all male poets in possession of the mother, the poetic 'muse'. Gilbert and Gubar interpose the woman writer into this archetypal male poetic tradition and conceive of her as being caught in the rupture of a two-fold creative angst, situated in a position so as to both encounter the resilient and domineering male precursors and their debasing and repressive representations of women on the one hand, and also to counter the insinuation that the act of writing is conspicuously and unrelentingly a male intellectual industry, on the other. If we look at what Gerard Manley Hopkins once wrote to his friend R.W. Dixon in 1886, we can clearly comprehend the cause of doubt and apprehension of 'literary women' having to confront this oppressively 'patriarchal theory of literature' and find out a locus of her own:

> The artist's "most essential quality", he declared, is "masterly execution, which is a kind of male gift, and especially marks off men from women, the begetting of one's thought on paper, on verse, or whatever the matter is." In addition, he noted that "on better consideration it strikes me that the mastery I speak of is not so much in the mind as a puberty in the life of that quality. The male quality is the creative gift."[3]

Gilbert and Gubar postulate that women authors do not experience the 'anxiety of influence' in a similar manner, as their male counterparts do, only because of the fact that they have to contend with their predecessors who are 'almost exclusively male, and therefore significantly different from her.' What is more oppressive to the female writer is her portrayal by male writers as being completely disconsonant with 'her own sense of her self':

> Not only do these precursors incarnate patriarchal authority ..., they attempt to enclose her in definitions of her person and her potential which, by reducing her to extreme stereotypes (angel, monster) drastically conflict with her own sense of her self – that is, of her subjectivity, her autonomy, her creativity.[4]

It is such a demeaning and immuring portrayal of her potential that she has to battle against. Gilbert and Gubar depict the struggle of the woman writer comprehensively:

> Her battle, however, is not against her (male) precursor's reading of the world but against his reading of *her*. In order to define herself as an

> author she must redefine the terms of her socialization. Her revisionary struggle, therefore, often becomes a struggle for what Adrienne Rich has called "Revision – the act of looking back, of seeing with fresh eyes, of entering an old text from a new critical direction ... an act of survival." Frequently, moreover, she can begin such a struggle only by actively seeking a *female* precursor who, far from representing a threatening force to be denied or killed, proves by example that a revolt against patriarchal literary authority is possible.[5]

Emily Dickinson, in her zealous accolades on other women authors,extolled their authority –a fact that implies that writers like Elizabeth Barrett Browning, George Eliot and Charlotte Bronte, are assimilated into the spiral of her own artistic perception. But Vivian Pollak, at the same time, puts forward the instance of Dickinson portraying Barrett Browning as the 'purveyor of illicit experience, as witch and magician.'[6] But the emotion Dickinson attached with the Barrett Browning is evident in Poem 312:

> Her – "last Poems" –
> Poets – ended –
> Silver – perished – with her Tongue –
> Not on Record – bubbled other,
> So divine –[7]

Joanne Feit Diehl examines Dickinson's poetic thought as such a 'performance of influence' which 'leads us to a provisional formulation of a paradigm that applies more generally to nineteenth-century women poets as they seek independence from powerful male precursors.'[8] Hence, for Dickinson, the predecessor evolves to become a composite masculine character and they find themselves descendents of an extensive line of forefathers who emerge as their antagonists. Hence, it is true that Dickinson's creativity was more often than not unequivocally encouraged by the women writers of the time whom she regarded as members of an authorial sisterhood and in whose works she took great interest. She took part in their success and gained resilience from them. It is worthmentioning here that Dickinson shared her works with her sister-in-law, Susan Gilbert Dickinson, more than with anybody else during her lifetime. Emily cared for Susan's opinions, but did not always adhere to her recommendations. In spite of her literary association with a protective sisterhood, the poet expresses her consternation regarding the yearned-for, yet minatory, male figure that possesses the authority either to devastate or to bestow life on the poet:

> I am afraid to own a Body –
> I am afraid to own a Soul –
> Profound – precarious Property –
> Possession, not optional –
>
> Double Estate – entailed at pleasure
> Upon an unsuspecting Heir –
> Duke in a moment of Deathlessness
> And God, for a Frontier.[9]

Emily Dickinson appears to have completely departed from Walt Whitman here. The subsuming strain and the effusion contained in his 'I am the poet of the Body and I am the poet of the Soul … The first I graft and increase upon myself, the latter I translate into a new tongue'[10] posits the greatest contrapuntal stance to Dickinson's proscriptions, retrogressions and abjurations. However, Dickinson's art, in many ways, betrays distinctive cultural tendencies that are quintessential and even axiomatic.

'Own[ing] a Body' or the poet's predicament of reification, a theme that this poem puts forward, is the pivotal philosophy that marks Dickinson's poetry. A significant array of invincible themes converges in her work. These include the concerns of identity that almost compulsively make her anxious. They encompass her identity as a woman poet, but the probability of, and the aspiration for, its 'embodiment in a text'[11] through language appears exceptionally equivocal due to a number of associated considerations such as, 'her identity as a woman, both in terms of inhabiting a woman's body and of womanhood as a figure for the body; her religious identity, in a broad metaphysical context of ambivalence towards material and temporal embodiment; and finally her identity as an American, in terms of definitions of selfhood as these have peculiarly taken shape within the history of the United States.'[12]

What is primarily noticeable in Poem 1090 is the dilemma and intransigence that mark its theme. As is often the case, any Dickinson text becomes more nebulous as one endeavours to decipher it. This element of textual profusion, unpredictability and heterogeneity in her poetry is efficaciously brought out in the following manner:

> This textual obduracy is, in many ways, in itself a central Dickinsonian subject. Dickinson poems require the closest textual attention. They cannot easily be cited as evidence in an argument, since closer textual work almost always uncovers further readings and implications not easily resolved or subsumed into a summary statement. This is the case both within and between Dickinson texts. It is one of the first tasks of Dickinson criticism exactly to acknowledge and consider this textual multiplicity in Dickinson's work, but less as indeterminacy or open-ended ambiguity or (only) aesthetic play than as the deployment and mutual confrontation between personal and cultural forces that are deeply at stake for her.[13]

Talking about such a cultural undercurrent, it is certainly difficult for the woman poet to continue with the flow of her creativity unhindered, and even uninfluenced, by the powerful male writings and, more importantly, those of her male literary predecessors. Within such an existing as well as a pre-existing masculine cultural framework, the woman poet has to encounter all the elementary, corporeal, legitimate and living circumstances as constituent elements comprising her life, death and the genesis of her artistic craftsmanship. Righteousness and incorruptibility are not a component of Dickinson's poetic self. Her poems provide a discourse on the inhibited occurrences in her life – the pivotal stages of time that are irretrievable. Initial experiences constrict her domain of a prospective enterprise. Exploring the period of her girlhood, Dickinson recollects no haven of approbation for herself. Indoctrinated to consider children as extinct humans who must acquire benevolence before they can be exonerated from culpability, she bears the sense of being expelled and proscribed from the *a priori* plausibility of such a state of bliss. She departs from the Romantics in not reminiscing about the 'visionary gleam' forgotten in the course of evolution, since she has seldom been allowed to experience it. When Dickinson imagines an Elysian ecstasy, anxiety betokens her consciousness. In one of her letters towards the close of her life, she wrote: 'In all the circumference of Expression, those guileless words of Adam and Eve never were surpassed, "I was afraid and hid Myself".'[14] For this reason, Dickinson's poems have often been correlated with William Blake's *Songs of Innocence and Experience*, but the contrast allows for an irrepressible incongruity. Dickinson voices her thoughts only about experience. Conversely, the poems which endorse an illusion of innocence are recognizably her most blistering observations. Discerning the sombre paradoxes, Clark Griffith comments that the poems that adopt an impersonation of innocence do so as a facade. It is through such contradictions and ironies, the ingenuous certitude is impugned.[15]

Sentiments reflecting anxiety constitute Dickinson's perception of human experience. The trepidation that she encounters while envisaging the inception of any prospective delight, emerges from an existing domain of cognition, a premonition that might be considered as the agonizing aggregate of the assurance life is expected to certify. Her scepticism of nature and her seclusion from mother and God emanate from this premeditated non-existent irreproachability; it hinges on an enlightened cognizance of the possibilities of trauma brought about by experience. In the core of this chiefly passionate strain, death and a prompt criticism of the divine law are ingrained:

> The life doth prove the precept, who obey shall happy be,
> Who will not serve the sovreign, be hanged on fatal tree.

The perception of this reality discernibly harps on the chords of impending death:

> The worm doth woo the mortal, death claims a living bride,
> Night unto day is married, morn unto eventide;[16]

Dickinson withstands the angst of an imminent jeopardy that constrains her to desist before acceding to circumstances of conceivable happiness as well as anguish:

> Come slowly – Eden!
> Lips unused to Thee –
> Bashful – sip thy Jessamines –
> As the fainting Bee –
>
> Reaching late his flower,
> Round her chamber hums –
> Counts his nectars –
> Enters – and is lost in Balms.[17]

She feels anxious since, to her, a receptive utterance – if inspiring and fascinating – is significant; else she apprehends that she might have to forfeit the impulse of perseverance that is needed to create. The voice of a transcensdental being primarily stimulates her and makes her conscious of her quiescence. This realization coalesces with both the spheres of her art and death. But this association is seldom congruent, 'for words themselves at once "enchant" and "infect" her'[18]:

> They carry a lethal potency akin to the attraction of death, which offers a solution to life's mysteries and the erotic satisfaction of sacrifice, giving one's self to an inscrutable lover. But death renders the soul silent, and communication between the dead and the living proves impossible.[19]

Dickinson's anxiety arises from the dilemma between the enchantment caused in her by death when she endeavours to forestall the malaise brought about by her experience of reality, and the consternation she feels from the debilitating reticence it prescribes.

As has been noted earlier, for Dickinson, the poetic precursor is a composite male figure whom she invokes, rather than obviates, in her act of creation. It is this invincible antecedent force that corroborates her conception of the muse. This identification between the poetic forefather and the muse simultaneously confounds and compulsively untangles her 'anxiety of influence'. The muse acquires significance and his ascendency is enhanced through this similitude. Hence, Dickinson's muse strikingly differs from that of the Romantics including Wordsworth, Keats and Shelley. Their muse is represented by the conventional image of an immaculate deity, who is a distant identity, conspicuously distinguishable from the poetic forefathers, who were sometimes fanciful forebears also. When Dickinson conceives of her muse as male, she is apprehensive of her own virile strength and avoids him with extreme disquietude, on the one hand, and desires to court him, on the other:

> We shun it ere it comes,
> Afraid of Joy,
> Then sue it to delay
> And lest it fly,
> Beguile it more and more –
> May not this be
> Old Suitor Heaven,
> Like our dismay at thee?[20]

Dickinson here delineates a characteristic instance of dramaturgy, wherein 'it' may allude to a phase of time, a paramour, or an imaginative spur.

An intensified anxiety overwhelms Dickinson when she acquiesces in a possible transposition in the subliminal consciousness, having experienced a change from her own condition of selfhood to that of a more formidable source of poetic inspiration. This psychic metamorphosis brings forth an apprehension that the docile obedience that she had proscribed may return if she abases herself to the male muse. This disquietude results in Dickinson's scepticism and her equivocal reactions towards the alien interloper in her poems. The poet experiences so intense a strain that she is prone to forsake her poetic aspirations and the faculty of performance. However, as a consequence of her encounter that is marked by patient resignation, comes the accomplishment of an exultant poet that is expressed through the following verse:

> I would not paint – a picture –
>
> ....
>
> Nor would I be a Poet –
> It's finer – own the Ear –
> Enamored – impotent – content –
> The License to revere,
> A privilege so awful
> What would the Dower be,
> Had I the Art to stun myself
> With Bolts of Melody![21]

Language, in this case, demonstrates the force of desire and dismay that informs Dickinson's perspective of self-sufficiency of the poet and the uncertainty associated with poetic autonomy. She affirms her individuality without any dependence on a governing male figure, though she appears to be perturbed by the possibility that she might be enfeebled as a consequence of which she would be rendered too powerless to create. Her poems vacillate between these two ends and hence the discord continues to remain entangled and finds articulation in her later poems:

> Growth of Man – like Growth of Nature –
> Gravitates within –
> Atmosphere, and Sun endorse it –
> Bit it stir – alone –
>
> Each – its difficult Ideal
> Must achieve – Itself –
> Through the solitary prowess
> Of a Silent Life –[22]

Evidently, these poems seldom allude to the theme of poetic creation, but the tendencies they reveal encompass the whole gamut of Dickinson's life and her experiences. The métier of the poet constitutes one of her cardinal considerations not only for the sole reason that she devoted her life to creating poems, but also due to the fact that she recognizes the faculty of the poet as having a sublime position above the corporeal world and the artistic enterprise as having a divine reverence. She asserts her prerogatives by saying: 'I reckon – when I count it all – First – Poets – Then the Sun –'.[23]

Dickinson joins the poetic tradition of perceiving the creative task as sharing similarities with the process of the birth of a child. She foregrounds the real experiences that such a course entails, though she does not associate the biological reality with poetic conception. At the same time, she emphasizes the pangs of physical challenges attendant upon artistic impregnation.

Dickinson manifestly endeavours to assume a male authority, perhaps because she perceives herself to be the one who has to hold back for the male. She adopts both masculine and feminine personas so as to embolden herself and to evade the perils of supine submission. How much she subscribes to a male identity understandably depends on the magnitude of her anxiety. In some poems, this masculine figure, be he God or father or a precursor poet, seems so inaccessible that he seems almost implausible, whereas in others, their supremacy perspicuously remains inherent. Such conceptualization posits its own uncertainty, since Dickinson is anxious about a disintegrated self over which she possesses limited sway. Such an association may be deleterious. It is pertinent to mention here that in a letter to Louise and Frances Norcross, Dickinson designates herself as 'brother Emily' which she uses as her signature.[24] In another letter to Edward Dickinson, she alludes to the counsels given to her by her mother when she was 'a Boy'.[25] Her 'chiefest apprehension' lies in the possibility of proving 'insufficient' in meeting the expectations of the stupendous task of her authorship:

Lest I should insufficient prove
For His beloved Need –
The Chiefest Apprehension
Upon my thronging Mind –[26]

Another cause that precipitates Dickinson's anxiety is her compulsion to confront this male master residing within, so that she may gain the necessary strength to expostulate against the angst that an encounter of two concealed identities brings about. She contemplates forbidding him primarily due to the adversarial elements of the forceful 'other' within her. But the attempt appears to her to be insurmountable:

Of Consciousness, her awful Mate
The Soul cannot be rid –
As easy the secreting her
Behind the Eyes of God.[27]

Whenever the conditions of selfhood and otherness in her conjoin to form one unified poetic self, it authorizes her to assume the distinguishable supremacy that she was once empowered with. This unification of the split self enables her to overwhelm the intimidating constraints that she feels within herself. Once she has gained the ability to reassure herself, she repudiates such a masculine other with a peremptory remark: 'Art thou the thing I wanted?/ Begone – my Tooth has grown –'.[28]

References

1. Elizabeth Barrett Browning, *The Letters of Elizabeth Barrett Browning*, 2 vols. ed. Frederic G. Kenyon (New York: Macmillan, 1897), Vol. I, pp. 231-32.
2. Harold Bloom, *The Anxiety of Influence: A Theory of Poetry* (New York and Oxford: Oxford University Press, 1973).
3. Gerard Manley Hopkins and Richard Watson Dixon, *The Correspondence of Gerard Manley Hopkins and Richard Watson Dixon*, ed. C. C. Abbott (London: Oxford University Press, 1935), p. 133, quoted in Sandra M. Gilbert and Susan Gubar, The Madwoman in the Attic: *The Woman*

Writer and the Nineteenth Century (New Haven and London: Yale University Press, 1979), p. 3.

4. Gilbert and Gubar, *The Madwoman in the Attic*, p. 48.

5. Adrienne Rich, 'When We Dead Awaken: Writing as Re-vision', in Barbara Charlesworth Gelpi and Albert J. Gelpi eds. *Adrienne Rich's Poetry* (New York: Norton, 1975), p. 90, quoted in *The Madwoman in the Attic*, p. 49.

6. Vivian Pollak, *Dickinson: The Anxiety of Gender* (Ithaca and London: Cornell University Press, 1984), p. 240.

7. All Emily-Dickinson Poems from 1 to 494 are taken from the following e-Source: *https://ia700301.us.archive.org/2/items/poemsofemilydick030097mbp/poemsofemilydick030097mbp.pdf* (Emily Dickinson, The Poems of Emily Dickinson, 3 vols. ed. Thomas H. Johnson [Cambridge, Massachusetts: Harvard University Press, 1955], Vol. 1 [Poems 1-494], Poem 312, p. 234.

8. Joanne Feit Diehl, *Dickinson and the Romantic Imagination*, (Princeton, N.Y. : Princeton University Press, 1981), p. 15.

9. Emily Dickinson, Poem 1090. All Emily-Dickinson Poems from 495 to 1775 are taken from the following e-Source: *http://archive.csustan.edu/english/reuben/pal/chap4/dickinson.html* (Thomas H. Johnson ed. *Complete Poems* [Boston: Little, Brown & Co., 1960], as a part of PAL: Perspectives in American Literature – A Research and Reference Guide, An Ongoing Online Project, Paul P. Reuben [copyright]).

10. Walt Whitman, *The Complete Poems* (New York: Penguin, 1975), Song 21, p. 83.

11. Wendy Martin, *Cambridge Companion to Emily Dickinson* (Cambridge: Cambridge University Press, 2002), p. 129.

12. Ibid., pp. 129-130.

13. Ibid., p. 130.

14. Emily Dickinson, *The Letters of Emily Dickinson*, 3 vols. eds. Thomas H. Johnson and Theodora Ward, No. 946 to Mr. and Mrs. E. J. Loomis in 1884 (Cambridge, Massachusetts: Harvard University Press, 1958), Vol. 3, p. 846.

15. Clark Griffith, *The Long Shadow: Emily Dickinson's Tragic Poetry* (Princeton, N. J.: Princeton University Press, 1964), pp. 17-73.

16. Emily Dickinson, Poem 1, p. 1.
17. Ibid., Poem 211, p. 148.
18. Diehl, *Dickinson and the Romantic Imagination*, p. 18.
19. Ibid., p. 18.
20. Emily Dickinson, Poem 1580.
21. Ibid., Poem 505.
22. Ibid., Poem 750.
23. Ibid., Poem 569.
24. *The Letters of Emily Dickinson*, No. 367, early October 1871, Vol. 2, p. 490.
25. Ibid., No. 571, about 1878, Vol. 2, p. 622.
26. Emily Dickinson, Poem 751.
27. Ibid., Poem 894.
28. Ibid., Poem 1282.

2

'... The Ecstatic Limit/ Of Unobtained Delight': The Woman Poet's 'Doubt and Dread' of Unconsummated Love

Emily Dickinson, in many of her poetic renditions, is replete with manifest commendations of the paradoxical ecstasies of such an agonizing renunciation. Hence, a number of readers, like Richard Wilbur[1] and others, have considered 'Sumptuous Destitution' as the most significant *leitmotif* of her art, as is also evident in the work of Emily Bronte, and George Eliot. Simultaneously, Dickinson happens to be an inebriate of *air*, and perhaps since she writes in a trance caused by such inebriation, she is often rapacious, splenetic and covertly or overtly intransigent. The expression 'sumptuous destitution' sounds daunting and almost presumptuous since it implies a certain amount of voluptuousness, the term having unequivocal implications though, that she is willing to indulge in, even in her penury.Who else can be as true and unswerving as these women authors who sang of renunciation as necessity's most exalted and glorious righteousness?

A divergent array of predicaments in describing female selfhood in and through language is demonstrated by Emily Dickinson. Her poems thematizing love are distinguished for their exceptional ingenuity:

> I gave myself to Him –
> And took Himself, for Pay[2]

But a thorough appraisal of such seemingly unpretentious avowals call forth, more often than not, inconsistent interpretations of rejection, paradox or a sincere longing proved unattainable by an inaccessible goal:

The Fruit perverse to plucking
    But leaning to the Sight
With the ecstatic limit
    Of unobtained Delight.[3]

When Dickinson speaks in the ecstatic or otherwise anguished first person that she makes use of in her love poems, she is so ambiguous and deceptive as to evade a conclusive explanation, and hence, the poems become conundrums often with two correspondingly possible responses. This is manifested in an acclaimed and contextually relevant poem:

Wild Nights – Wild Nights!
  Were I with Thee
Wild Nights should be
  Our luxury!

. . . .

Rowing in Eden –
  Ah, the Sea!
Might I but moor – Tonight
  In Thee![4]

This ardent poem expresses a yearning for someone whose nearness indicates a threatening and an almost impulsive intemperance as well as an absolute detachment from unsettling upheavals – significances that coherently gainsay one another. 'Wild Nights should be/Our luxury!' stimulates a release of forcefulness perceived as a forbidden act of reprobation, but it is completely uncertain whether the 'luxury' implies the outburst of a passionate ardour or the assurance of a concealment from it. Corresponding inconsistencies are to be fathomed in the second stanza also: 'You are "done with the compass" when you are safe at home.' The exuberance contained in the line calls to mind a relinquishment so consummate that the speaker, in spite of being stranded in the midst of the ocean, is no more anxious about where she exists. Contrarily, the connotation of 'Ah, the Sea!' is conjectural. The enigma it evokes centres round the question whether the sea symbolizes her lover or separates her from him. If the tempest and the sea exemplify a passionate vitality by the use of 'I', they can seldom clearly illustrate the portents she hopes to overpower. This tantalizing indeterminacy is a characteristic of a more perplexing poem:

> The Drop, that wrestles in the Sea –
> Forgets her own locality –
> As I – toward Thee –
>
> She knows herself an incense small –
> Yet *small* – she sighs – if *All* – is *All* –
> How *larger* be?
>
> The Ocean – smiles – at her Conceit –
>
> But *she*, forgetting Amphitrite –
>
> Pleads – "Me"?[5]

This aphoristic anecdote of the 'Drop', encouraged by love to struggle for her own individuality, is designed on an antithesis. The intricate central stanza appears to demonstrate the dilemma of self-expression. If she acknowledges that the ocean, being boundless, 'is All', or in other words, if it already subsumes her, how, 'she sighs', can she magnify it? She imperiously desires that the ocean should be immeasurable without taking her into consideration. This demand appears grotesquely presumptuous from the point of view of the fact that the sea has consumed more voluminous matters in comparison to what she could do and it is not inappropriate to distinguish it or him as the sea-god, Poseidon, who already has a wife, the sea-nymph named Amphitrite. It may however seem surprising to discover how such an endeavour of self-expression is intrinsically associated with selfless love and the self-submission that comes from it. The reader's experience of the poem remains one of contradiction. Dickinson's poems of love remind us of Andrew Marvell's 'Definition of Love' where love is 'begotten by Despair/Upon Impossibility'.

Such poems on despair may be hailed as some of Dickinson's most admirable accomplishments. In 'There's a certain Slant of light', despair comes out thoroughly and conclusively:

> There's a certain Slant of light,
> Winter Afternoons –
> That oppresses, like the Heft
> Of Cathedral Tunes –[6]

'Heft' implies heaviness, with supplementary associations of dragging, exertion and pressure. The 'Cathedral Tunes' become burdensome due to the sombre strain of certitude and demand to be lifted up by the hearers. These suggestions traverse back through a sense of oppression to the winter-afternoon 'Slant of light', that is apparently immaculate, yet dispassionate. Dickinson brings these implications together naming them as despair, which she again describes as 'An imperial affliction/Sent us of the Air –':

> When it comes, the Landscape listens –
> Shadows – hold their breath –
> When it goes, 'tis like the Distance
> On the look of Death –

Death comes from the distance and, hence, the two share an intimate association in many of Dickinson's poems, where the non-existence of the lover bears the sensation of death. Distance is impregnated with all possibilities of an impending fatality and such solitude provides the poem with a death-like finality.

Love manifests itself in Dickinson's poems in multifarious forms. It is perceptible that she loved intently, rapturously and unswervingly in her life. She sometimes loved exuberantly and, at other times, sedately. She also habitually transcended restrictions. She vacillated between one way of loving and the other just in the manner she dithered to determine expressions that would befit a poem. She cruises along effortlessly across widely assorted attitudes, dispositions and circumstances, creates poetry by the fervour of her imagination, and enacts a vivacious playfulness from an entirely fantasized notion of love. She was indisputably aware of the way in which she could assume the role of a passionate companion, paramour and devotee. She confided to one of her childhood friends, in the concluding year of her life, that she perceived and even 'this moment knew – / Love Marine and Love Terrene – / Love celestial too –'.[7] She spread her love to every domain of life that she could envisage.

The anxiety in Dickinson arises from the fact of her sustained adherence to a prototype that concedes to a binary hierarchy, where the subject is unquestionably the male and the object female, in spite of the fact that a female speaker speaks in these love poems. This seldom implies that the female persona identifies her subjectivity as male; the speaker here, in fact, tries to strike a balance between the dominant male subject and his female 'counterpart' by considering herself as an object. In the following poem, she conceives of a garden, unchanged and yet 'brighter', a place where she urges her endearing brother, Austin, to come from the land where he is:

> Never mind faded forests, Austin,
> Never mind silent fields –
> Here is a little forest,
> Whose leaf is ever green;
> Here is a brighter garden,
> Where not a frost has been;
> In its unfading flowers
> I hear the bright bee hum:
> Prithee, my brother,
> Into my garden come![8]

It is language that reinforces the position of the subject and the object, and ushers in the essence of a heterosexual intrigue. This amorous strain, underlying the relationship between the 'female subject' and the 'male object' (the subversion as is perceivable in the above-quoted verse) is embedded in the patterned metaphorical structure of the poem that is manifestly grandiose and far-ranging. A few familiar comments on the inherent meaning of this interrelationship between romance and metaphor probably indicate the reason why this correlation enhances the dilemma that Dickinson confronts as a female poet. Acceding to the argument of Jacques Lacan,[9] the French psychoanalyst, that subjectivity is comprised of and by language, and that to imbibe language is to concede to the social and cultural norms, particularly those that bear witness to patriarchal authority, the French feminist critic Luce Irigaray debates that the hierarchical taxonomy of a signifier and a signified in language reiterates and underpins the subjugation of women and their treatment as object.[10] Irigaray asserts that metaphor characterizes the edifice of language. It pivots on and propagates a hierarchical system of polarization in which one constituent element possesses the prerogative to determine the other. Irigaray's views are in accord with the explanations of Sigmund Freud[11] and Lacan that the position of the woman in this metaphorically designed system of language is basically that of absence, of a deprivation, and the components of language that restate the elements of presence and absence actually, in their turn, replicate the reality of marginalization of women. Hence, when Dickinson deploys the theme of subject-object relationship through the use of such metaphor, she virtually anticipates that by which Irigaray was intrigued.

The thematics of romantic love characterizes Dickinson's early love poems, particularly those that reveal such an ideal of love, expressed with the help of metaphor in which the subject-object relationship receives a vivid manifestation. In her later love poems that were composed several years after her early compositions, and which comprise the verse valentines of 1850 and 1852, and the rhyming end of a letter to Austin in 1851 identified by Thomas Johnson as her second poem, she conceives of ideas as both corroborating and offering a critical assessment of a hierarchical association that lovers share in her earliest poems. In this category of her poetry, the self is considered as nugatory, feeble and womanly and is juxtaposed against an array of authoritative, evidently male, representations, as distinctively expressed in the poem, 'Mute thy Coronation –',[12] where the speaker is a 'meek' and deferential 'tiny courtier' who conceives of herself as being shrouded in the master's 'Ermine' on the event of his coronation. The diminutive steward appropriates herself in the position of the object, and the metaphorical strain of absence in the hierarchical paradigm of romantic attachments is depicted in a manner in which the menial and the exiguous is desired by the powerful and the significant in the initial valentine. But, in other poems composed almost around the same time, Dickinson endorses a subversive assessment of traditional romantic affinities between the male and the female through a concurrent appraisal of the two-fold organization of language and metaphor. Dickinson envisages a relation between the subject and the object that is imperative to both the schemes of metaphor and romantic love, and essentially to those of signifier and signified that language depicts.[13] It is strikingly noticeable that in her efforts to redress this adversarial pattern of language, Dickinson forces language to the verge of inconsequentiality. Her endeavours to untether the binary opposition of subject and object in romantic associations have confronted corresponding hindrances. As a result, one particular section of her poems seems to conform to the design of the traditional love poems, which can be identified in her earliest poems and persists in the later poems like 'Mute thy Coronation –', to name just one of them. In this section of poems, the dominant male persona, who embodies the characteristic features both of God and of the father, is portrayed as the sun, whereas the frail and insubstantial female self is imagined as a daisy. This traditional constitution of bipolarization, echoing the conventional male-female relationship found in the earlier love poems, is substantiated only to be later disintegrated. Simultaneously, the metaphor that is rudimentary to such an idea of polarity, and is indispensable to the frame of these stereotypical relations, is nonetheless challenged and undone.

In the love poem, 'The Daisy follows soft the Sun',[14] the daisy transposes the ostensible association between supremacy and deference in romantic love, and the metaphor that underpins the design of the poem, along with the relationship it delineates, is unfolded as a misapprehension:

The Daisy follows soft the Sun –
And when his golden walk is done –
Sits shyly at his feet –
He – waking – finds the flower there –
Wherefore – Marauder – art thou here?

The discrepancy between the sun and the daisy, that is essential to their relationship, is metaphorically expressed in a way similar to that in the poem about the Master and the petite courtier. Dickinson tries to draw a parallelism between the daisy and the sun particularly because of a superficial similitude that is evident in the former's name, the 'day's eye'. Such similitude deepens and the flower, whose very name signifies the eye of the day, is described by an analogy in relation to the sun. The effort to unite the remarkable incompatibility between them exemplifies their romantic enchantment as well as the metaphor that presides over the poem. The discernible image that as the sun draws near the horizon, the daisy 'follows soft the Sun' and 'Sits shyly at his feet', bears testimony to the way in which both metaphor and intrigue are at function in the poem through language. It is again with the help of such language that the poet creates an artistic delusion, making the daisy resemble the sun and their relationship seem close and affectionate.

As Dickinson steers towards a clearer and more archetypal culmination of a male-female love intrigue, she presents marriage as a 'soft eclipse'. The speaker here presumes herself as having experienced 'the Girl's life' and rounds off by saying:

This being comfort – then
That other kind – was pain –
But why compare?
I'm "Wife"! Stop there![15]

When one assumes the role of a wife, it is imperative for her to 'stop'. Stopping implies a cessation in the growth of a woman's life as well as the fact that the poem reaches its finale. Rather than declaring an end to all the apparent contrasts between the conditions of being a wife and those of being a girl, the poem suggests a startling reticence as a substitute for such comparisons.

Though the language here enforces a peremptory silence, Dickinson seldom stops. She remains in a perpetual pursuit to diversify the confines of the observable, the conceivable and the explicable both in experiential and in linguistic terms, though, for her, feeling the physical reality in her mind is virtually the same as experiencing it by actually living it. The essence of Dickinson's poetry is constituted of the rapture and gratification of an amorous male-female relationship where the language bears evidence of a metaphor that comprises an indeterminable dilemma of the signifier and the signified. Hence, love evolves as a symbol of a subjugating force underpinned by such a metaphor that augments that force.

If such a restrictive paradigm of romantic love of the opposite sexes calls for a language that is itself oppressive, constraining and, hence, sometimes nebulous, it may seem plausible that such an affinity between women might hypothetically suggest a felicitous form of experience communicated through a more convenient, germane and expressive language.

The individuality that Dickinson puts forward in her letters was perceptibly male as much as being female. Yet, it is sometimes formidable to allow for such a transformation in poems. Dickinson sent 274 poems to Susan Gilbert Dickinson, primarily her friend and subsequently her sister-in-law, apart from 154 pieces of prose correspondence. Such poems and missives are manifestly self-explanatory since they establish a relationship of uniformity as far as the question of gender is concerned or, in other words, unravel an attempt to disrupt the notion of a hierarchical order by specifying a relationship between two women. The language deployed to convey the intricacies of such a kinship is therefore one that is structured on an identical condition of selfhood, rather than a conclusive experience of detachment. The ideological accent in the poems involving two female personae is clearly on equivalence and homogeneity, perhaps reinforcing the sense of a considerable number of Dickinson's poems as revealing homoerotic closeness. Seldom can such a consanguinity between two congruent units be categorized as conforming to the demands of a hierarchical strategy, none of them being more pronouncing than the other. However, it is perplexing to note that instead of demonstrating a restful equipoise that such a circumstance may presupposingly foster, these poems are typified by Dickinson as having the problem of no imaginable conclusion because of the specific sameness of the two identities concerned. Poem 642 expresses on the one hand, 'We're mutual Monarch', and on the other, 'Myself – assault Me'. Consequently, poem 683 reveals the metaphor of 'the most agonizing Spy' by saying that, 'The Soul unto itself / Is an imperial friend – / Or the most agonizing Spy – / An Enemy – could send –'. Other poems concerning two corresponding female figures apparently bear a similar framework and are based not on contrariness and polarity but on consistency and interchangeability, thus often leading to an acute and an overwhelming impasse.

However, there are both conveniences and hindrances in such poems that delineate both the subject and the object as female, as in the case of 'Like Eyes that looked on Wastes'.[16] Such an approach reveals both the affirmative and the negative aspects of life as well as of language. The penultimate lines of the poem, 'Neither would be a Queen / Without the other –', reveal this poem to be an interaction between two female characters, though this poem was not one of those dispatched to Susan. There is, arguably, no possibility of any idea of a hierarchy owing to the fact that none either *is* or *is not* a queen. Yet, a perception of an appalling lack becomes clearly discernible. The poem begins with a sustained analogy between 'Eyes that looked on Wastes' and the manner in which the two personae behold one another. There seems to be a corresponding requital of observation among them:

So looked the face I looked upon
So looked itself – on Me –

Here the subject-object polarity ceases to exist and their images produce indistinguishable mirror reflections:

But Blank – and steady Wilderness –
Diversified by Night –

Just Infinites of Nought –
As far as it could see –

The poem concludes with a combination of contradictions arising from this reciprocal gaze:

The Misery a Compact
As hopeless – as divine –
Neither – would be absolved –

Neither would be a Queen
Without the Other – Therefore –
We perish – tho' We reign –

The dearth of a difference makes this 'Compact' 'hopeless' and from this insufficiency, neither of them can find liberation. The culmination proves to be even more disconsolating since both of them 'perish – tho' We reign'. The uniformity in the nature of their being precludes them from transposing their condition of existence, which again appears to be threatened by a situation of stalemate. Metaphor, here, rather serves as an avenue, enabling a kind of circumvention of such a situation of impasse, than merely being a literary device of language.

Both love and poetry bring for Dickinson a calamitous end. Her love poems are seldom considered as objective demonstrations in relation to the form of traditional lyric poetry. In Dickinson, the correlation between God and the 'lover-bridegroom' becomes 'too persistent to be dismissed' and certainly involves associations of male involvement and female dis-eases. Albert J. Gelpi cogently asserts that 'love was for her an experience which had something to do with man and something to do with God .... The association of the amatory and, in a loose sense, the mystical – as God becomes lover-bridegroom or lover manifests preternatural or deific qualities – is too persistent to be dismissed'.[17] Such an experience finds expression in the following poem:

> Struck was I, not yet by Lightning –
> Lightning – lets away
> Power to perceive His Process
> With Vitality.
>
> ....
>
> Most – I love the Cause that slew Me.
> Often as I die
> It's beloved Recognition
> Holds a Sun on Me –[18]

Initially mutilated by an unusual assailant, Dickinson comes out from this ordeal being enthusiastic for more scars. She asserts having undergone such tribulations as could be compared with a mortal assault and eventual death. It is as if she redeems her 'Power to perceive His Process', and then takes delight in the reiteration of her death. Though she feels numbed by being deprived of a lover who 'Holds a Sun' on her, Dickinson seems defaced in his companionship. As he withdraws from her, his dominance dwindles and she identifies in his retreat the moment of her regeneration.

References

1. Richard Wilbur, 'Sumptuous Destitution', in Richard B. Sewall ed. *Emily Dickinson: A Collection of Critical Essays* (Englewood Cliffs, N. J.: Prentice Hall, 1963), pp. 127-36.
2. Emily Dickinson, Poem 580. All Emily-Dickinson Poems from 495 to 775 are taken from the following e-Source: http://archive.csustan.edu/english/reuben/pal/chap4/dickinson.html (Thomas H. Johnson ed. *Complete Poems* [Boston: Little, Brown & Co., 1960], as a part of PAL: Perspectives in American Literature – A Research and Reference Guide, An Ongoing Online Project, Paul P. Reuben [copyright])

3. *Ibid.*, Poem 1209.
4. Emily Dickinson, Poem 249, p.179. All Emily-Dickinson Poems from 1 to 494 are taken from the following e-Source: *https://ia700301.us.archive.org/2/items/poemsofemilydick030097mbp/poemsofemilydick030097mbp.pdf* (Emily Dickinson, The Poems of Emily Dickinson, 3 vols.ed. Thomas H. Johnson (Cambridge, Massachusetts: Harvard University Press, 1955), Vol. 1 [Poems 1-494]), Poem 249, p. 179.
5. *Ibid.*, Poem 284, p. 203. Poet's italics.
6. *Ibid.*, Poem 258, p. 185.
7. Emily Dickinson, *The Letters of Emily Dickinson*, 3 vols. ed. Thomas H. Johnson (Cambridge, Massachusetts: Harvard University Press, 1958), Letter no. 975 to Mary Warner Crowell, dated early March 1885, Vol. 3, p. 865.
8. Emily Dickinson, Poem 2, pp. 2-3.
9. Jacques Lacan, *The Language of the Self: The Function of Language in Psychoanalysis* (Baltimore: The Johns Hopkins University Press, 1968).
10. Luce Irigaray, 'Women's Exile', interview by D. Adlam and C. Venn, trans. C. Venn, in *Ideology and Consciousness* 1, Paris: Minuit, 1977, pp. 62-76.
11. Sigmund Freud, *The Interpretation of Dreams*, trans. A. A. Brill (New York: Macmillan, Third Edition, 1913); Published online by Bartleby.com in August 2010.
12. Emily Dickinson, Poem 151, p. 108.
13. Margaret Homans, "Oh, Vision of Language!": Dickinson's Poems of Love and Death', in Suzanne Juhasz ed. *Feminist Critics Read Emily Dickinson* (Bloomington: Indiana University Press, 1983), pp. 114-33.
14. Emily Dickinson, Poem 106, p. 80.
15. *Ibid.*, Poem 199, p. 143.
16. *Ibid.*, Poem 458, p. 353.
17. Albert J. Gelpi, *The Tenth Muse: The Psyche of the American Poet* (Cambridge, Massachusetts: Harvard University Press, 1975), pp. 241-42.
18. Emily Dickinson, Poem 925.

3

Judge Tenderly of Me:
The Woman Poet in Quest of Succour in Nature's 'Tender Majesty'

An Everywhere of Silver
With Ropes of Sand
To keep it from effacing
The Track called land.[1]

Emily Dickinson's scholastic cognition of language, however, is perceivably best exhibited in her contemplation of this natural and experiential world. The enthusiasm with which Dickinson celebrates Nature – the spectacles and the manifestations – was, as the expressions corroborate, so much a concern of immense importance as to impinge on the poet's thought and cognizance. She proves to be most accomplished, proficient and erudite in depicting how she observes things to be. She examines both the deep-seated investigations of avant-garde poetry and those of conventional lyric. She closely considers 'the Outside' and the 'in' (Poem 1097, c. 1866) of objects and efforts to demonstrate the correlation between the two. She substantiates the presence of the beholder and occasionally enables the onlooker to interpolate the objects s(he) visualizes. We do comfortably fathom that she takes delight in the reflections of Nature and feels ecstatic to versify them through her poetry.

The cited lines from Poem 884 invoke almost an immaculately convivial sensation. The poet's individuality does not interpose the silvery 'everywhere' which suggests a mysterious mode of silence. There is an imperturbable serenity in the moon-blanched landscape with the placid water in the midst, with a consciousness that peace is ephemeral. But the objects themselves preponderate. 'In a poem of this sort', as Ezra Pound remarked of his own imagist verse, 'one is trying to record the precise instance when a thing outward and objective transforms itself or darts into a thing inward and subjective.'[2]

Dickinson's mode of versification was most venerated by the propounders of the Imagist Movement, which had a constructive influence on the progress and maturation of modern poetry. Her representation of the humming-bird, distinguished for moving twice as swiftly as other birds, is reiteratively adduced as a remarkable prototype of explanatory writing:

A Route of Evanescence
With a revolving Wheel –
A Resonance of Emerald –
A Rush of Cochineal –
And every Blossom on the Bush
Adjusts its tumbled Head –
The mail from Tunis, probably,
An easy Morning's Ride –

In addition to the above illustration, Dickinson's observation of a humming-bird has found expression in the following manner:

Within my Garden, rides a Bird
Upon a single Wheel –
Whose spokes a dizzy Music make
As 'twere a travelling Mill –

But He, the best Logician,
Refers my clumsy eye –
To just vibrating Blossoms!
An Exquisite Reply![3]

The aura of human individuality, intrinsic in imaginative writings, is primarily subdued in the richly embellished revelation of the 'Resonance of Emerald', the iridescent and psychedelic humming-bird along with its reverberations, its alacrity and its impetuousness. Hence, the quick-witted reflection of the observer is astonishing and as felicitous and germane to an acknowledgement of the quiddity of the midget bird as the representation itself. Both the bird and the beholder precipitatingly dissolve into the silence, resigning with vibrating resonances that fill the landscape. There is no other poem that Dickinson was so selective about consigning to her correspondents. It appeared first as a poem associated with the oriole and the essence of thought, 'I hope they are not untrue', in a correspondence to Helen Hunt Jackson in 1879. In early 1880, the poet dispatched a transcription of the poem to her friend and neighbour, Mrs. Edward Tuckerman, who was also the wife of the Professor of Botany at Amherst College and the sister-in-law of Frederick Tuckerman, himself a poet. In November 1880, Dickinson conveyed it along with three of her other poems with the perspicacious solicitation, 'Reprove them as your own', to Thomas Higginson. She also communicated a copy to Mabel Loomis Todd in October 1882 and to Thomas Niles in April 1883.[4]

A poem, the rubric and exegesis of which can be expunged without emasculating the effect of the imagery, predisposes, by comparison, to forfeit its fervency and enthusiasm. Creating in the nineteenth century, Dickinson could not remain unsusceptible to making sporadic utterances, but she maintained a quotidian and succinct pattern. In a poem, delineating the bat, to take a specimen, the equipoise is impeccably preserved. She enunciates, without pronouncing so, 'Behold, the only mammal that can fly!'

The Bat is dun, with wrinkled Wings –
Like fallow Article –
And not a song pervade his Lips –
Or none perceptible.

His small Umbrella quaintly halved
Describing in the Air

An Arc alike inscrutable
Elate Philosopher.[5]

She has not merely glimpsed at the bat, but she has keenly contemplated on the palpitating animal with all its idiosyncrasies. She takes a punctilious heed of the fact that the bat's sonority is so acute in its amplitude that it becomes inaudible to the human ear and also that it can aviate even in darkness. An expressive veracity of language and a ratiocinative and percipient ecstasy in the convolution of this perplexing world are the imperatives to compose poetry as an enraptured onlooker who neither thrusts upon us a saturnine depiction of the bat, nor incubates the creature. Hence, transforming it into an idealized personification would be to elevate both the bat and the poem in its entirety over the accepted modes of thought and representation in imagist poetry.

A poem Dickinson once christened as 'a chill Gift' (the poet included the poem as 'a chill Gift – My Cricket' in a letter of mid-March 1883 to Thomas Niles, L, 3: 768) coalesces the subtleties of the images with the exuberance of the one who partakes of the sedate pageantry of Nature:

Further in Summer than the Birds
Pathetic from the Grass
A minor Nation celebrates
Its unobtrusive Mass.

Remit as yet no Grace
No Furrow on the Glow
Yet a Druidic Difference
Enhances Nature now[6]

The departing Summer, solemnized devoutly according to institutional practice by its commemorators, conjures up a deep cogitation and a 'Druidic Difference' that give an impression to the poet which is more impregnable with the myriad reflections of the season, but this is true only if one undertakes to circumscribe the imagery in order to be visually perceptible as well. The clamour and squawking of 'the Birds/Pathetic from the Grass' and innumerous incognito aphids and microbes constituting 'A minor Nation' are phantasmagoric in their mysterious audibility without being visibly present. The sensory intelligibility of the poem is predominantly and recognizably aural, with the regurgitating orchestration and the jarring timbre quivering in the aural membrane. These are petty resonances – unostentatious onomatopoeic tones – yet they are as much in propinquity as the remorseless music of 'A minor Nation' is to the natural environs, the resounding pulsations of which are synchronous and at once importunate, tranquil and fretful. By way of experiencing this multi-echoing choir, it is possible to presuppose that August is burning pianissimo. The bucolic faith consists of the idea that when such sounds are heard for the first time, frost is going to be six weeks away. The sultry effulgence of the intensely simmering twelfth hour and the chirpy cicadas 'Pathetic from the Grass' will herald the winter, along with its snowy confederates and other modes of quiescence and serenity, which is, in its turn, analogous to the plaintive strains of the 'spectral Canticle' enhancing 'Nature now'.

The essence of Dickinson's nature poetry is that her verse exhibits a blend of an experienced Romantic inner perspicacity and scrupulously perused empirical natural spectacles and occurrences, a mélange which capacitates her to create beyond elementary and graphically ornate poems. The impeccability of language describing the 'Winter Afternoons' is surprising in that it voices the enigmatically inscrutable transience and impermanence of life:

> There's a certain Slant of light,
> Winter Afternoons –
> That oppresses, like the Heft
> Of Cathedral Tunes –
>
> When it comes, the Landscape listens –
> Shadows – hold their breath –
> When it goes, 'tis like the Distance
> On the look of Death –[7]

We feel that the strain of the tacit incandescence, sprinkled throughout the winter sky, is equally weighty as the 'Heft / Of Cathedral Tunes'. In spite of the fact that both the 'Slant of light' and the 'Heft' are not onerous, they are certainly repressive, since they portray 'a certain Slant' and 'Tunes' that actually augur the grim and portentous ordeal of seclusion and along with it an indubitable cosmic placidity. The 'Shadows', constituting the 'Landscape', 'hold their breath' in apprehensive pre-emption. The 'listening landscape' seems to prognosticate 'the look of Death' in 'the Distance'. The imagery of the poem, in its entirety, is a promulgation of the experience of life, the reclusivity of the very being of man and is the pronouncement of the fact that all figurations and metaphorical typifications of the universe are hallowed, yet gainsay the existence of a final and decisive significance which mortal sensory perceptions can descry beyond the terminal destination of death.

Dickinson preferred realistic details of portrayal of the beatific magnificence of Nature using unorthodox and outré personifications. She imagines of 'An Antiquated Tree' treasured by the crow in 'Corporation Coat' (Poem 1514, c. 1881), equates 'The splendor of a Burmah' (Poem 1466, c. 1879), or affirms that 'Glass was the Street – in tinsel Peril / Tree and Traveller stood –', but contrarily states that, 'Hearty with Boys the Road - // Shot the lithe Sleds like shod vibrations' (Poem 1498, c. 1880). She enunciates with equivalent verve:

> A Bird came down the Walk –
> He did not know I saw –
> He bit an Angleworm in halves
> And ate the fellow, raw,
>
> And then he drank a Dew
> From a convenient Grass –
> And then hopped sidewise to the Wall
> To let a Beetle pass –[8]

Dickinson writes from the stance of an onlooker and develops the object, which is 'A Bird' in this poem, with personifying traits of an individual and bestows upon 'him' a distinctive attribute to which the poet reciprocates.

Several other images and visualizations of natural phenomena do enamour her and the uniqueness of her verses on Nature is that such spectacles also conspicuously articulate the effervescence and vivacity with which she refurbishes etiolated phraseology with lively enthusiasm. One is effortlessly prone towards explaining a sunset less as something redundant than as a light that is 'sparkling' or 'fading'. She records the impressions of a momentous American sunset presenting it as being in semblance with an itinerant band of circus men who had wrapped up their tents and 'dissolved' 'utterly' to some other country:

I've known a Heaven, like a Tent –
To wrap its shining Yards –
Pluck up its stakes, and disappear –

No Trace – no Figment of the Thing
That dazzled, Yesterday,
No Ring – no Marvel –
Men, and Feats –[9]

Dickinson revelled in cavorting with apparently unexceptional, but ethereal experiences as an aureate sunset. Her witticisms and her ingenious repartee are exceptionally singular and free from the callowness and insufficiency of premature composition:

I never told the buried gold
Upon the hill – that lies –
I saw the sun – his plunder done
Crouch low to guard his prize.

That was a wondrous booty –
I hope 'twas honest gained.
Those were the fairest ingots
That ever kissed the spade!

She marauds the terms and questions, 'Whether as I ponder/ Kidd will sudden sail –'.[10]

It is almost customary to describe the forest terrain enveloped with the long needle-shaped leaves of the pine trees as merely being 'a thick layer of woven fabric.' But Dickinson's response sounds in the following manner:

Of Brussels – it was not –
Of Kidderminster? Nay –
The Winds did buy it of the Woods –
They – sold it unto me

It was a gentle price –
The poorest – could afford –
It was within the frugal purse
Of Beggar – or of Bird –

She demonstrates the 'small and spicy Yards' and 'the hue' as 'a mellow Dun'. She envisages the 'carpet' to be constituted of 'Sunshine – and of Sere –' but most importantly 'of Sun' which 'The Wind – unrolled' 'fast' 'And spread' 'on the Ground' (Poem 602, c. 1862).

Hence, in spite of the fact that Dickinson may ostensibly seem to repudiate the existence of a transcendental divine identity, her reflections on the impermanent and evanescent objects of Nature do give us the perception that she works towards mortalizing the visions of the phenomenal world in order to construct a cosmic identity and demonstrate its stupendous majesty, sublimity and glory. She does indeed frolic among such familiar and undistinguished sights and surroundings, and in the process of metaphorizing them, leaves an implicit supplication for some space in the midst of the natural world in which she can create. She arduously remains in quest for meaning and neither accedes to the singularity of purport nor to the implication of human existence. It is this ceaseless interplay of multitudinous teleological variables existing behind this perpetual flow of human life that bewilders and mystifies the poet and she rationalizes her puzzlement and strives to discover new meanings by moving from one object to the other, be it the cheerful cricket, winter afternoon, a golden sunset or the forest floor. This constant process of relocation precipitates anxiety in the female poet who earnestly solicits consolation and relief from the scruples and disquiet of authorship. We see Dickinson departing from the Romantics, both ideologically and thematically, since she neither glorifies nor idealizes Nature in the manner her Romantic progenitors did, nor does she present a magnanimous poetic self that resigns completely from natural sights and sounds and submits to the Supreme Saviour.

In her seminal work, *Women Writers and Poetic Identity: Dorothy Wordsworth, Emily Bronte, and Emily Dickinson,* Margaret Homans has traced the Wordsworthian thesis of 'feminization of nature' and the idea of 'Mother Nature' as 'the object of poet's love' and 'the necessary complement to his imaginative project':

> William Wordsworth's feminization of nature is the most obvious example of sexual polarization in the literary tradition that would have shaped women poets' conception of poetry. When nature is Mother Nature for Wordsworth, she is valued because she is what the poet is not. She stands for a lost memory, hovering just at the edge of consciousness, of a time before the fall into self-consciousness and into subject-object relations with nature, whether that original unity took place in earliest infancy or, fictively, before birth. As the object of the poet's love, Mother Nature is the necessary complement to his imaginative project, the grounding of an imagination so powerful that it risks abstraction without her.[11]

This Romantic presence of a 'mother' in the Nature the poet aspires to poetize, is actually perceived as 'a son's mixture of devoted love', but more significantly, as 'resistance to the constraints, she would place on his imaginative freedom'.[12] This unambiguously indicates that she would be nothing above and beyond what he desires her to be. It can nonetheless be unsurprisingly expected that the feminist critical and historical agenda would undeniably subsume the philosophy of a matriarchal community that preceded the polarized and dichotomous patriarchal structure existing in Egypt and Greece followed by western culture afterwards. The origin of this matriarchy can be traced in the manner Homans does:

> This matriarchy is generally described as originating in the worship of fertility, in which the earth is a mother goddess and all nature, including humanity, is her creation and her domain.[13]

What is actually relevant here is the agreeability and acceptability of the idea to sustain the matriarchal notion, whether fictive or historically factual, in the manner of subscribing to the fact that women can be veritably and indistinguishably commensurate with men in competence and authority. But there is an essential division between women and the theme of 'matriarchization'. The maternal conception of Nature, as pioneered by Wordsworth, and its deification can barely be placed in apposition to the abilities of women themselves or even to the real everyday happenings in their lives. Homans goes to the extent of arguing that, 'Whether as a cultural or political memory, or as personal myth transmitted into poetry, Mother Nature is not a helpful model for women aspiring to be poets. She is prolific biologically, not linguistically, and she is as destructive as she is creative.'[14]

But not all Dickinson's poems that thematize Nature corroborate what Homans contends. She composes a poem in six stanzas deploying Mother Nature as a necessary motif:

> Nature – the Gentlest Mother is,
> Impatient of no Child –
> The feeblest – or the waywardest –
> Her Admonition mild –[15]

The fundamental question that arises here is, whether the metaphor of a mother's warm and tender care and affection, being infinite is an enunciation of Nature's true portrayal of her motherly traits or a depiction of the specific qualities symptomatic of the paragon of motherhood or an implication of the poet's own mother.

The poem is scarcely impersonal and dispassionate. The poet also delineates the turbulent storm and misfortune Nature is afflicted with in the same manner in which she gives a deprecating account of her mother. The description is perhaps rather emotional and nostalgic particularly in a circumstance, with the poet herself not having a mother, a fact that is no more than a veritable truth. There are personal elements depicting the attributes of Emily Norcross Dickinson in Emily Elizabeth Dickinson's passionate individualization of Nature, an examination which is not wholly impeccable in its details, neither truly in the case of Nature nor in that of the poet's mother. The fervently passionate child shares some of the qualities with her mother in her youth, something that is evidently manifest in her letters. It is perhaps due to this sense of depletion and unfulfilment to obtain motherly care and concern that there are present certain elements of discernible wilful intransigence in her poems:

> A Drunkard cannot meet a Cork
> Without a Revery –
> And so encountering a Fly
> This January Day
> Jamaicas of Remembrance stir
> That send me reeling in –[16]

Dickinson was extensively following the tradition of literary practice considerably formulated by Ralph Waldo Emerson[17], a convention that perhaps outdistanced Wordsworth's unimpeachable and reverent observations on Nature. Emerson was, in actuality, more egotistical in contrast to the British Romantic philosophers, but his magnification of this poetic stance proved felicitous for Dickinson, the female-poet-inheritor. His self-subsuming theorization takes a nugatory cognizance of the discriminatory identity of the 'non-self' and this has convenienced Dickinson's poetics since she is not resisted by the corresponding implacable and mythical metaphor of the female individual self and her hopes and aspirations. Liberated, as Emerson's self-inclusive thought is, it adopts an asexual stance since the notion of this almost austere inclusivity unequivocally entails a disencumbering exclusion from demarcating any object identifiable by sexuality. Dickinson's use of rhetoricity rather than her portrayal of Nature as mother with 'tender majesty' brandishes her femaleness and underpins her rage and restlessness as a female poet allowing her to construct an evolutionary poetics of Nature that not merely departs from, but stands in acerbic distinction to the epochal 'Mother Nature' engendered by the Romantics, who responded to the son in a way that the daughter's voice remained unheard and inconsequential. Dickinson took up this theme of the hitherto peripheralized and unuttered song of the daughter poet by contemplating a hermeneutic construct that, through apparently atypical and unorthodox metaphorization, transubstantiates the objects of the natural world which, in their turn, thus emerge as a poetic correlative to the ideal and transcendental world.

There are poems that betray the tranquillity and quietude that she finds in Nature. Such an instance of self-composure is revealed in the peroration of the following poem:

> Image of Light, Adieu –
> Thanks for the interview –
> So long – so short –
> Preceptor of the whole –
> Coeval Cardinal –
> Impart – Depart –[18]

When the poet hearkens 'a shouting Flower / The proclamation of the Suns' (Poem 1519, c. 1881), 'Winter instantly becomes / An infinite Alas –'. At another place, she reflects with an equanimity that is emblematic of autumn. She examines phlegmatically, 'The Cricket drops a sable line / No more from yours at present' (Poem 1635. c. 1884) and the vivaciously human 'Mountains straight reply' to the corporeal and natural world constituted of words. The words are elusive to the poet and she ceaselessly goes on with her quest for proper forms of expression to depict her observations of the experiential world from the stance of a woman poet, to whom words are thus the objects of experimentation towards achieving self-expression.

Arriving at the context of language, Jacques Derrida's poststructuralist thought concerning 'phallogocentrism' is pertinent here. The overarching eagerness to remain poised at the centre is conspicuous in its identification with the phallus and with the 'Word'. The centre, due to its immensity and far-fetchedness, is rhetoricized as an 'enormous and old root'.[19] Derrida coalesces his construct of 'logocentrism' with that of Lacan's 'phallocentrism'. The quintessence of Derrida's logocentric thought is constituted of a distinction between 'logos' representing voice and that characterizing writing. Here, we can scarcely overlook the fact that the term 'logocentrism' is deployed in apropos of logos in a more traditional perception of language. The speaker or the writer is privileged to remain positioned at the centre whereas the female is conceived of as contorted and temperamental, as an aberrant human. In concordance with Derrida's substantiation of the association between the pen and the phallus, writing is required to be predisposed and understood in reference to phallocentrism. The word is enhancingly segregated from its signification owing to an endless deferral of signifiers reinforcing the fact that there is no fixed or transcendental signified. Hence, in this interminable process of deferment, the word comes first, seconded by its postponed meaning. Nietzsche feels that woman's 'castration' occasions her to represent the 'lack' or 'absence', the absence or the necessary implication to which the word drives forth.[20] Derrida discreetly calls attention to the unwarranted ascription of the idea of woman to the true form of female existence in the physical world in a study concerning Lacan whom he extracts in order to cite at the conclusion of the following excerpt:

> Phallogocentrism is one thing. And what is called man and what is called woman might be subjected to it .... Androcentrism ought therefore to be something else.

> Yet what is going on? The entire phallogocentrism is articulated from the starting-point of a determinate *situation* ... in which the phallus *is* the mother's desire inasmuch as she does not have it .... The sequel is familiar: phallogocentrism as androcentrism with the whole paradoxical logic and the reversals which it engenders: for example that 'in the phallocentric dialectic, she [the woman] represents the absolute Other'.[21]

Hence the 'woman', owing to her lack, is relegated to the periphery as being 'the absolute Other'. But Lacan's metaphor of the 'Other' can be appropriated with the idea of the 'necessary implication' which, though appears to be a 'lack' in the already-uttered meaning, is actually the reinforcing truth.

The signifier-signified divergence in Deconstruction may therefore tend to dismantle the phallogocentric idea, impeding feminist thought in a decidedly unsettling manner. The theme of the 'logos', when manoeuvres to produce meanings, unfolds the literal ones indicating fixed identities of signification, while antithetically, this objective is understood to be unencompassable and unattainable owing to the endless deferral of signifiers within a sign system. Due to this dichotomy existing in the theme of the 'logos', men were not placed enough affirmingly in a position from where they can deploy words as constituent elements of an uninterrupted and unalloyed whole, but women indubitably discerned the specific predilection of the way in which language was employed in the Bible. This predilection consisted of a disentanglement of women writers from the phallogocentric commune, and this disengagement from the centre stimulates Dickinson to strive for a separate and an individualized form of language and thereby to create a hitherto unconstructed pattern of the self. Hence, we feel that the enterprise denoted rather a reprisal against a tendentious centre than an affirmation of a positivist thought, more for this invincibly dominant poet than perhaps what it sometimes did for Christina Rossetti or Elizabeth Barrett Browning. Dickinson dissents from the preconceived system of language with all its predilections and proclivities and, in the process, nullifies the conventional denotations of words and expressions.

The reprehensible and disparate characteristic of language that Dickinson most persuasively impugns is the hierarchy present in the system, and her most effectual accomplishment as a conscientious female poet lies in her cognition that this categorization is embedded in the core of male ascendancy. A centripetal force towards literary dominance brings about an oppressive thought so much so that the non-partisan notion of resistance, both linguistic and sexual, tends to be in conformity with such a hierarchy, since one component has to be prioritized over the other in order to garner the prerequisites of such a bigoted sequentialization. Deliberating on Nietzsche's contentions on women, Derrida primarily demonstrates that Nietzsche's 'eternal war between the sexes' is 'based on what might be called a process of propriation', and then adds that 'propriation is all the more powerful since it is its process that organized both by the totality of language's process and symbolic exchange in general'.[22] The extract serves to polarize the concepts of language and sexual discrimination while Derrida evolves a construct of reversal of the hierarchical order. He opines that language functions so as to recognize the 'Other' as 'self', to expropriate the object and reconstruct it as the subject. Adamic speech, putatively impeccable since the meanings correspond to the words, is also a pattern of arrogative language, since Adam used language to signify supremacy over the creatures he nominated and he named the woman as well.

Though Emily Dickinson endorsed the philosophical overtones of Emerson's supposition that the universe is an embodiment of the soul, she reformulated the thesis and postulated that the mind of a genius effectuates and sculpts the supple veneer of Nature. In the manner of a self-solipsist poet and in noticeable distinction with a metaphysicist, she astutely transferred her accent from a prodigious power that occupied her to her potency to acquire Nature. This perspectivist transformation is successfully manoeuvred, for instance, in the following poem:

Perception of an object costs
Precise the Object's loss –
Perception in itself a Gain
Replying to its Price –

The Object Absolute – is nought –
Perception sets it fair
And then upbraids a Perfectness
That situates so far –[23]

According to Dickinson, so enormous in strength is the poet's perception that it 'sets' 'fair' the object, which is no more than a 'nought'. Such perceptive power reprimands a 'Perfectness / That situates so far –'. Hence, the remotely distanced 'Perfectness' is of little consequence to the poet, whose epistemological acumen renders 'Precise the Object's loss –', thereby being commensurate with inconsiderable mortal survival. Magnificently vocal, yet subtle, as Dickinson was, she triumphantly proclaimed her power as a poet to ascertain meaning, an act not to be determined either by Nature or the experience of it:

To hear an Oriole sing
May be a common thing –
Or only a divine.

So whether it be Rune,
Or whether it be none
Is of within.

The "Tune is in the Tree –"
The Skeptic – showeth me –
"No Sir! In Thee!"[24]

The valour of the poet's subjectivity enables her to recognize the 'Tune' within so much so that she can encounter the daunting challenges of Nature. This inner melody overawes the outer natural entities in majesty and resplendence. Dickinson, as a female poet, realizes the inconceivable power of the innate 'red' 'Fire' of creation and metaphorizes not the eerie enchantment of the lightning, but the conflagrating élan submerged deeply in the volcano of the poet's perception:

How red the Fire rocks below –
How insecure the sod
Did I disclose
Would populate with awe my solitude.[25]

As a corollary to this, she refrained from obtrusive representation of an explosion preferring to keep it simmering inside the unfathomable chasm:

The reticent volcano keeps
His never slumbering plan –
Confided are his projects pink
To no precarious man.

Admonished by her buckled lips
Let every babbler be
The only secret people keep
Is Immortality.[26]

The perplexity caused by the dilemmatic internal and external power also finds expression, though equivocally, through implications of timorous feminine consciousness. At one time, she yearns for her Master's encouragement and patronage, elsewhere she winces at him acceding to his dominance and still at other times, she finds herself overhauled by the natural phenomena she observes with great care and circumspection. Her anxiety concerning her poetic position lies in these irreconcilable arguments, where she makes a perceptible feminine supplication to the authoritarian master on the one hand, and herself takes mastery over Nature and thrusts on it her own association of meanings, on the other. Her early poems also broach this dilemma through connotations of the flower and the bee – symbols and figures which, through various modes of representations, allegorize the poet's authorial agnosticism.

The flower, in most circumstances the rose or the daisy, craves to touch the divine 'Conditions' by itself standing 'negative':

... till the Bee
Blossoms stand negative,
Touched to Conditions
By a Hum.[27]

The incessant thrumming resonance performs an instantaneous mesmerism and the verdant exemplar is transformed into a refulgent rose:

A sepal, petal, and a thorn
Upon a common summer's morn –
A flask of Dew – A Bee or two –
A Breeze – a caper in the trees –
And I'm a Rose![28]

Dickinson identifies herself with a blossom, particularly a rose, only to realize with distress that 'to be a Flower, is profound/ Responsibility', and she frequently carps that the bee is, in actuality, a duplicitous Lord, an erratic paramour who adored her only to forsake her so much so that she has to survive without divinity:

His Suit a chance
His Troth a Term
Protracted as the Breeze
Continual Ban propoundeth He
Continual Divorce.[29]

At other times, Dickinson prefers to envisage herself as the bee swigging from Nature's 'Velvet Masonry', an action which soon becomes his high prerogative so much so that he is transformed into a supremely proficient and experienced creature having the power to overwhelm, subjugate and impregnate the torpid eventuality:

Like Trains of Cars on Tracks of Plush
I hear the level Bee –
A Jar across the Flowers goes
Their Velvet Masonry –

Withstands until the sweet Assault
Their Chivalry consumes –
While He, victorious tilts away
To vanquish other Blooms.[30]

Dickinson, as a poet, could envision herself both as the bee and as the flower, the captivator and the captivated. She perceived both the stances equally well and it is perhaps this act of dual impersonation that demonstrates her disquiet and qualm as a conscientious and perspicacious woman poet:

Because the Bee may blameless hum
For Thee a Bee do I become
List even unto Me.

Because the Flowers unafraid
May lift a look on thine, a Maid
Alway a Flower would be.[31]

In yet another poem, 'The Bumble Bee's Religion' (Poem 1522), the poet both commiserates with the Bee and simulates the flower. But, as a result, the initial proposition, 'All Liars shall have their part', execrates the bee's perfidious act of defloweration, while the latter assumption, 'And let him that is athirst come', gives credence to the flower's solicitation.

If the poet contrives more towards envisaging herself as the bee, she, at a point of time, completely attains an authoritative presence that capacitates her with invincible potency. Dickinson presupposes that the office of the poet consists of the act of bringing out an '... amazing sense / From ordinary Meanings – / And Attar so immense / From the familiar species / That perished by the Door –',[32] as well as of wringing the unexceptional rose so that the 'Attar so immense' can be obtained:

Essential Oils – are wrung –
The Attar from the Rose
Be not expressed by Suns – alone –
It is the gift of Screws –[33]

In this portrayal of poetic manoeuvre with customary representations, the rose emerges out to be an epitome of the constituent elements that comprise the natural phenomena. The sun symbolizes the paramount source of nourishment and the attar, the creative purgation. Dickinson, thus, professes a new poetics, departing noticeably from both Barrett Browning and Rossetti, in which she refuses to perceive art as a primary imitation of phenomenal events or as the process of evolution of a creative muse through inspiration, traditionally believed to be something true to the poet's imagination. Instead, she understands it as a palpable human progression from genesis to extinction in which the poet acts as the 'sublimator' of the natural objects she sees and experiences. The artist requires to have the concerned education, adroitness and dexterity to perform her artistry and hence it is the craftsman as the performer of her task who wrenches 'The Attar from the Rose'.

To Dickinson, Nature appeared to be 'a Haunted House', an esoteric storehouse of significance, which it is the artist's contrivance to engender. More often than not, the observation emerges out to controvert the ideology of transcendence, leaving the artist with a more commanding stance of 'inventing' implications from such an arcane, cryptic and recondite repository of art and knowledge:

> Nature assigns the Sun –
> That – is Astronomy –
> Nature cannot enact a Friend –
> That – is Astrology.[34]

The woman poet's impassioned supplication comes to us in a revealing manner. The anxious and distraught artist communicates to an unknown audience of the future for her creation to be judged with due introspection, sensitivity and solicitude. She feels ostracized from the world she writes to, since she believes that the 'tender' and majestic Nature has conventionally belonged to a stringently defined male literary territory and has still not been completely explored and investigated by her art:

This is my letter to the World
That never wrote to Me –
The simple News that Nature told –
With tender Majesty

Her Message is committed
To Hands I cannot see –
For love of Her – Sweet – countrymen –
Judge tenderly – of Me[35]

References

1. Emily Dickinson, Poem 884. All Emily-Dickinson Poems from 495 to 775 are taken from the following e-Source: http://archive.csustan.edu/english/reuben/pal/chap4/dickinson.html (Thomas H. Johnson ed. *Complete Poems* [Boston: Little, Brown & Co., 1960], as a part of PAL: Perspectives in American Literature – A Research and Reference Guide, An Ongoing Online Project, Paul P. Reuben [copyright]).
2. Ezra Pound's classic imagist poem, 'In a Station of the Metro', consists of two lines. The first draft of the couplet, according to Pound, was thirty lines long. Hugh Kenner, The Pound Era, Berkeley and Los Angeles: University of California Press, 1971, pp. 184, 197.
3. Poem 500, c. 1862.
4. Emily Dickinson, *The Letters of Emily Dickinson*, 3 vols., eds. Thomas H. Johnson and Theodora Ward, Cambridge, Massachusetts: Harvard University Press, 1958, vol. 2, pp. 639-40; vol. 3, pp. 655, 681, 741, 769-70; vol. 2, p. 545.
5. Emily Dickinson, Poem 1575, c. 1876.
6. *Ibid*, Poem 1068, c. 1866.
7. Emily Dickinson, Poem 258, p.185. All Emily-Dickinson Poems from 1 to 494 are taken from the following e-Source: *https://ia700301.us.archive.org/2/items/poemsofemilydick030097mbp/poemsofemilydick030097mbp.pdf* (Emily Dickinson, The Poems of Emily Dickinson, 3 vols.ed. Thomas H. Johnson (Cambridge, Massachusetts: Harvard University Press, 1955), Vol. 1 [Poems 1-494]), Poem 249, p. 179.

8. *Ibid*, Poem 328, p. 261.
9. *Ibid*, Poem 243, p. 175.
10. *Ibid*, Poem 11, p.14.
11. Homans, Women Writers and Poetic Identity. Dorothy Wordsmith Emily Brothers and Emily Dickinson, (Princeton, N.J. : Princeton University Press), p. 13.
12. *Ibid.*, p. 13.
13. *Ibid.*, p. 13.
14. *Ibid.*, p. 13.
15. Emily Dickinson, Poem 790, c. 1863.
16. *Ibid.*, Poem 1628, c. 1884.
17. Ralph Waldo Emerson, T*he Journals and Miscellaneous Notebooks of Ralph Waldo Emerson*, vol. VIII, 1841-3, eds. William Gilman and J. E. Parsons, Cambridge, Massachusetts: Harvard University Press, 1978, p. 87.
18. Emily Dickinson, Poem 1556, c. 1882.
19. Jacques Derrida, 'The Purveyor of Truth', in *Graphesis*, Yale French Studies, 52, 1975 (pp. 31-113), p. 96, translated from 'Le Facteur de la verite', *Poetique*, 21, 1975, pp. 96-147.
20. Jacques Derrida, 'La Question du style', in *Nietzsche aujourd'hui?*, Paris: Centre Culturel de Cerisy-La-Salle, 1973, I, pp. 235-287; also published in a four-language edition, translated into English as *Spurs: Nietzsche's Styles*, trans. Barbara Harlow, Venice: Corbo e Fiore, 1976.
21. *Graphesis*, pp. 98-99.
22. *Spurs*, pp. 85-87.
23. Emily Dickinson, Poem 1071.
24. *Ibid.*, Poem 526.
25. *Ibid.*, Poem 1677.
26. Poem 1748.
27. *Ibid.*, Poem 1042.
28. *Ibid.*, Poem 19.
29. *Ibid.*, Poem 896.
30. *Ibid.*, Poem 1224.

31. *Ibid.*, Poem 869.
32. *Ibid.*, Poem 448, p. 346.
33. *Ibid.*, *Ibid.*, Poem 675.
34. *Ibid.*, Poem 1336.
35. *Ibid.*, Poem 441, p. 340.

4

'Why – Do They Shut Me Out of Heaven?': Female Ire and the Poetics of the Religious

> One of the most ardent female champions of women's rights has said that it is high time that the woman's side of religion should be heard from the pulpit, that men have too long had the monopoly, and have set the masculine aspect of Christianity too exclusively and persistently forward. Begging the lady's pardon, I cannot but think that the exact contrary is the truth. To me, judging from the sermons I have heard and read, and the devotional books I have examined, it is precisely the feminine way of regarding theology, and not the masculine, which is in the ascendant amongst us .... The broad fact is that a negative and unprogressive faith is usually taught, and that by all schools alike. The shibboleths may vary in accent, but they are all pitched in the treble cleff, and one does long for the mighty bass of a masculine theology.[1]

In the above-quoted passage, the author R.W. Littledale tries to convince the male reader that women would have been accepted as being far more affable had they been educated in religion and spirituality, as such knowledge would have helped to save them from those fastidious and facetious charges from which they never could virtually retrieve themselves. To put it more appropriately, 'women often jar against the sensitive nerves of men'.[2] Tradition has ever defined domesticity as being a woman's domain with utmost stringency. The need is to distort the uni-accented shibboleth of an ascendant masculine theology and associate divine wisdom with her domestic role. Littledale in *The Religious Education of Women* is clearly apprehensive about the concept of the feminine in theology – a factor which Lynda Palazzo argues with consummate appropriateness as 'what promises to be a document on women's religious emancipation is ultimately oppressive'.[3] Christianity had such a high-pitched male overture that it had virtually driven critics, to whom the fallacy did not wholly belong, to infer that the idea of the feminine can be, we hardly realize with what extent of the perception of subjugation, associated with 'inferiority' and 'weakness'.[4] What Littledale understands as 'the feminine way of regarding theology' is regarded by Palazzo as 'simply a projection of the way the male-dominated Church would like women to relate to theology'.[5] But what we see here is that the so-called 'virile' Church did not limit its masculine preachings to only what or how women would perceive theology, but set up a societal framework at large which would unconditionally be governed by such a 'male' concept of divinity.

It is true that Littledale was sympathetic in his attitude to women's grievances in theosophical matters, to be precise. More so, the ambition surrounding 'the feminine way of regarding theology' is clearly evident when he maintains that such a belief 'is in the ascendant amongst us ...' He asserted with a radical tenor that to confine the ideology of Christianity within narrowly defined masculine bounds is to develop 'a negative and unprogressive faith'. Hence, his disposition can, with undoubted correctness, be referred to as being contrastive of that of most of the well-known High Church figures. He goes on to maintain that the religious education imparted at the time was tyrannously unilateral in the sense that it deprived women of 'wholesome and harmonious development' and hence 'the purpose of God' is deliberately counteracted and threatened.[6] Palazzo substantiates the problem by putting it aptly in the following manner:

> ... stripping a prospective convent sister of ties of affection and of possessions is repressive and 'is an effort to crush out the affections and the ties of association' in themselves necessary to avoid 'selfism' and to promote 'altruism'.[7]

In a discussion on the right to religious education of women, the Miltonic reverberation of 'He for God only, she for God in him' remains unconflicted, reflecting femininity as a part of the image of God. With this divine feminine image in mind, Littledale claims that women 'should be strong, true, liberal, wise, and just'. He also felt the importance of them having the 'capacity trained into practical efficiency and decisiveness; like the noble portrait in the last chapter of the Book of Proverbs'.[8]

In an interesting study entitled *Reclaiming Myths of Power: Women Writers and the Victorian Spiritual Crisis*, Ruth Jenkins refers to a movement which evolved from the exclusion of women from divine and 'sacred authority'.[9] It 'attempted to resurrect the female aspects of God', and prognosticated even 'a female messiah, tapping the historic privilege Christianity had given the oppressed to challenge the world'.[10] The wealth of significant critiques on the issue also includes Florence Nightingale who borrowed from the Old Testament prophetic tradition, 'revised the incarnation to include female oppression',[11] and went to the extent of urging 'potential female prophets to herald the coming of a new Christ, "perhaps a female Christ"'.[12] She was a disbeliever of the established masculine doctrine of religion and hence accused the Church of England as having distorted 'the character of God'.[13] This ideology eventually led her to give birth to her own 'liberation theology'[14] concerning the sanctity of devoting oneself to nursing. The work of J. Ellice Hopkins is nonetheless reminiscent of what our present concern is constituted of. She reclaimed 'female sacrality through the sisterhood in her work among London's prostitutes'. She found 'spiritual relief' in being able to 'undermine the male monopoly on the administration of the sacred' 'by identifying personally with Christ in her mission to rescue desecrated womanhood'.[15] Hopkins emerged as another 'foremother of contemporary Christian feminism'[16] in her attempt to 're-enact' and 'redeem the role of Christ'[17] particularly at a time when women were excluded by the Church from priestly activity. Given this historical backdrop, we can revert to the theme of conceptualization of religion as an expressive mode to ventilate feelings of anxiety of authorship.

Emily Dickinson's epistemological doubt and her resulting poetic indeterminacy do not happen to her retroactively as a result of current critical conformist practices. Rather, they bear testimony to her personal doubts concerning religious faith and the gradually augmenting uncertainty, indefiniteness and restlessness of the age in which she composed her poetry. Doubt and desire impelled, rather than inhibited and discouraged, Dickinson's epistemological and poetic pursuit and she wished her song to continue to be heard. An early poem sets the theme of suffering and anguish she experiences on earth, which she visualizes from heaven. She delineates her experience of the Cross and her sense of its meaning in her 193rd poetic rendition composed around 1860:

> I shall know why – when Time is over
> And I have ceased to wonder why –
> Christ will explain each separate anguish
> In the fair schoolroom of the sky –[18]

She looks at the sufferings and agonies on earth from an exalted and elevated pedestal of heaven and her conception of Christ, in perhaps stark contrast to Rossetti, barely has eschatological dimensions. Hence, her image of Christ is strikingly, if not mundanely, human. She approved of and was interested in the sermon about the disappointment of Jesus in Judas, since it was 'told like a mortal story of intimate young men'. In a late poem, 'The Saviour must have been / A docile Gentleman –,'[19] and in an elegy on Charles Wadsworth, a charismatic Presbyterian Reverend, whom Dickinson admired deeply, the poet wrote:

> 'Twas Christ's own personal Expanse
> That bore him from the Tomb –[20]

Christ's 'personal Expanse' signified for her his triumph over suffering and it is particularly in this way that Dickinson tries to identify her artistic consternation and dilemma and the pain it entails, as endured by the Saviour. On the other hand, the Risen Christ or the Christ, the Consoler or Redeemer, does barely rouse her concern, since it is not the act of apotheosizing that she endorses, but it is Christ, the human sufferer, in whom she acquiesces comfortably. The mood of admonition and remonstration is conspicuous and clearly discernible in the opening lines of an undated poem:

> One crown that no one seeks
> And yet the highest head
> It's isolation coveted
> Its stigma deified[21]

It was the truth in a 'look of Agony' and 'the fashions – of the Cross –' that pierced her. According to her greatest crucifixion poem, she narrates the experience in a strangely familiar tone:

> One Crucifixion is recorded – only –
> How many be
> Is not affirmed of Mathematics
> Or History –[22]

Whenever she thought of abstemiousness, asceticism, fortitude, endurance or renunciation – that 'piercing Virtue' – or of the 'Thorns' she will assume 'till Sunset', or of 'the strong cup of anguish brewed for the Nazarene', she reverted, not so much to the Gospels as to the 'Imitation' with its authoritative accent on the renunciation of the world, shouldering the encumbrance and bearing the Cross, that is, adopting the unpretentious, austere and obdurate life of the committed and dedicated religious:

> To put this World down, like a Bundle –
> And walk steady, away,
> Requires Energy – possible Agony –
> 'Tis the Scarlet way
>
> Trodden with straight renunciation
> By the Son of God –
> Later, his faint Confederates
> Justify the Road –[23]

Dickinson's faith of the religious becomes pronouncingly felt when she speaks of reading 'with straight renunciation / By the Son of God –'. She identifies herself with the 'faint Confederates', renouncing the World 'like a Bundle' and 'walk[ing] steady away' the path wrought with artistic pain and agony. She followed the tormenting path of the woman author to its bitter end through 'straight renunciation' of the 'Scarlet way' that prohibits woman's creation thereby finding solace in the fullest commitment to the religious: 'Even in Our Lord's "that they be with me where I am"', she wrote, 'I taste interrogation.'[24]

She underwent an acute sense of suffering which was caused by a disavowal of the male literary tradition and was compelled by 'a loss of something' to bemoan 'a Dominion' of lost, if not forgotten, childhood. But, more often than not, a stroke of 'Suspicion' causes interruption to her search for 'delinquent Palaces' that she feels gravitating towards the 'site of the Kingdom of Heaven'. The poem,[25] indicated here, can also be understood to possess a little different, in other words, supplementary referral. Her religious anxieties came early as reflected by the above poem and it affected her profoundly. Girded by some devout and pious friends, she felt herself to be 'cast out', being 'the only Prince' and a 'Mourner' 'among the children'. She was perhaps afflicted by some strange spiritual lack which impelled her to conceive of Christ rather as a human figure than as a transcendental and divine being. Contrarily again, 'Suspicion' intervenes and she begins her search 'for the site of the Kingdom of Heaven'. But, retrospection and the nostalgic memory of childhood are again fraught with danger, if offered as a solution to the anxieties and discomforts of the present.

Noticeable in Elizabeth Barret, this disavowal of the matrilineal heritage of tradition affects Aurora Leigh as well Browning's *Aurora Leigh* when we find her orphaned of her mother during her early infancy. This can perhaps be understood in terms of an acutely felt absence or a lack of the sense of 'mother' in Barrett Browning's poetry. Similar was the state of affairs with the poet's life as well. So powerful was the emphatic influence of her father on her poetic abilities that she almost, occasionally, felt shocked by his presence, an experience which also, at the same time, inspired and enthused her to try to make her voice heard through her passionate and fierce commitment to create.

Dickinson also enters into the conventional reality of Christian devotion, as suggested by Oberhaus: 'The Bible pervades her mind of art, as it does the mind and art of all Christian devotional poets and writers. And the Bible was not, as many have supposed, merely a source of imagery for her. Rather, the Bible is essential to her structure and meaning, the very sum and substance of her art.'[26] The 'singularly cryptic' poems of Fascicle 40, says Oberhaus, require the reader to 'enact the role of sleuth'. This done, she sees 'F-40 as an architectural tour de force, a three-part meditation, a letter addressed to the reader, a garland of praise, and a conversion narrative, as well as the triumphant conclusion of the protagonist's account of her poetic and spiritual pilgrimage from renunciation to illumination to union and finally, after many conflicts, to contentment with this union.'[27]

This all the more amplifies the fact that the Christian metaphysical tradition unmistakably and ineluctably finds expression in her poetics, and operates interminably. Dickinson seldom completely dispossesses herself from the Christian, and particularly Calvinist, milieu in which she was brought up in Amherst, attaching to it often contentiously. The ceaseless metaphysical exigencies in her poetry are felt from the specific mode of juxtaposition of poems with a discernible religious dislocation or dissension and poems of a palpable religious fervour and complaisance. This argument, of course, does not identify Dickinson as a 'religious poet' nor does her quintessential and all-encompassing poetic understanding, derived from her sense of dispossession, raise her to a state of transcendence. 'She is, instead', says Jane Donahue Eberwein, 'a poet of religious engagement, whose very criticism of religion reflects her deep involvement in it.'[28]

Dickinson revelled in formulating a human image of God which sometimes dissuades us from her religious inclinations, if not her religious affiliation. Poem 251, being apparently simplistic, has implicit metaphysical intonations:

Over the fence –
Strawberries – grow –
Over the fence –
I could climb – if I tried, I know –
Berries are nice!

But – if I stained my Apron –
God would certainly scold!
Oh, dear, - I guess if He were a Boy –
He'd – climb – if He could!

What seems strikingly noticeable in Dickinson's religious thought is the concept of God being either a male or a 'female' idea. The expressions, 'if He were a Boy' and '... if I stained my Apron – / God would certainly scold!', portray respectively male and female images but, in both cases, they are very mundanely human. Similarly, in a later poem, the abode of such a 'human' God is conceived of as having an anthropomorphic existence. The poet raises some fundamental ontological questions, but does not quite seem to navigate into them so far as to extricate any comprehensible or a so-called 'human' solution to them. She subscribes to a description which is distant from a glorified or a chivalric idealization of the concept of 'Heaven', since she has not experienced it hitherto. The poet, hence, asks:

We pray – to Heaven –
We prate – of Heaven –
Relate – when Neighbors die –
At what o' clock to heaven – they fled –
Who saw them – Wherefore fly?
Is Heaven a Place – a Sky – a Tree?[29]

Perhaps the most revealing of her experiences of heaven, that received a mature enunciation, appears in one of her letters to Mrs. J. G. Holland during early August, 1856: 'My only sketch, profile, of Heaven is a large, blue sky, bluer and larger than the biggest I have seen in June, and in it are my friends – all of them – every one of them – those who are with me now, and those who were "parted" as we walked, and "snatched up to Heaven".'[30] She goes on to describe 'God' as an 'Old Neighbor' with much convenience and ease:

> How excellent the Heaven –
> When Earth – cannot be had –
> How hospitable – then – the face
> Of our Old Neighbor – God –[31]

All these human depictions can possibly be extrapolated as the poet's desire to be in propinquity with God, a hominid presence, who is more able to provide her with the solace and reassurance that she is desperately in need of. The 'Old Neighbor' can share and participate with her in her times of woe, despair, dejection and anguish much more conveniently than a distant, transcendental Omnipresence.

Dickinson deploys variegated themes and conceptualizes God in multiple and myriad images. At one time, she is roused by a revealing realization:

> God is a distant – stately Lover –
> Woos, as He states us – by His Son –
> Verily, a Vicarious Courtship –
> "Miles", and "Priscilla", were such an One –[32]

At another place, God is 'Revelation's limit' in the following manner:

> Embarrassment of one another
> And God
> Is Revelation's limit,
> Aloud
> Is nothing that is chief,
> But still,
> Divinity dwells under a seal.[33]

Through these diverse portrayals of the divine, Dickinson tacitly accedes to the fact of the eternity, truth and omnipresence of the divine being:

The Only News I know
Is Bulletins all Day
From Immortality
The Only Shows I see –
Tomorrow and Today –
Perchance Eternity –
The Only One I meet
Is God –[34]

The vastness and immeasurability of the 'Infinite' is delineated in contradistinction to God as a human image. The irreconcilable and antithetical conceptions become strikingly vivid when she says elsewhere:

They leave us with the Infinite.
But He – is not a man –
His fingers are the size of fists –
His fists, the size of men –[35]

God as an epitome of truth is also nonetheless telling in the following poem:

Truth – is as old as God –
His Twin identity
And will endure as long as He
A Co-Eternity –[36]

The above-quoted instances from Dickinson's poems may leave us with the consciousness that she acknowledged the predominance of a male divine figure with the reverberative 'He' or 'His' to designate such an image. But this dichotomous and incompatible angst as a woman writer pulls Dickinson apart and she does not, in any sense, miscarry her expression and this is how she asserts with vehemence and resilience:

To be alive – is Power –
Existence – in itself –
Without a further function –
Omnipotence – Enough –[37]

The poet endeavours and struggles for creative expression, an artistic enterprise that has, with equal vigour and constraint, agitated her mind. Dickinson apprehensively expresses her disquietude and malaise by disclosing that:

> My Worthiness is all my Doubt –
> His Merit – all my fear –
> Contrasting which, my quality
> Do lowlier – appear –[38]

Dickinson ventilates her ire firmly enough by loudly asserting that religiosity is presupposed to be inclusive of the idea of femininity which can scarcely be proscribed from the tyrannically defined 'angelic', or in other words, a male definition of religious participation. She debates with rancour and wrath:

> Why – do they shut Me out of Heaven?
> Did I sing – too loud?
> But – I can say a little "Minor"
> Timid as a Bird!
>
> Wouldn't the Angels try me –
> Just – once – more –
> Just – see – if I troubled them –
> But don't – shut the door![39]

'Protomodernist, proto-*verslibrist*, protoprojectivist, protofeminist'[40] Dickinson solicits these taxonomical structures for her poetry, through which she barely postulates any dogmatic propositions, bearing underlying convictions, philosophical ideas and pedagogical views. Such predilections on the part of the critics actually gainsay the quintessence of Dickinson's nature. Some critics have expostulated that Dickinson's early religious recalcitrance in reality paved the path for her subsequent contemplative and meditative certitude but in spite of such innate metamorphosis, she never preached a principle or a precept of any kind whatsoever. She reveals in a letter of February 13, 1859, to Mary Emerson Haven that 'Mr. S. preached in our church last Sabbath upon "predestination", but I do not respect "doctrines", and did not listen to him, so I can neither praise, nor blame.'[41] If we are to ascertain an unmistakable tinge of religious, aesthetic and ontological consideration in her poetry, she did opt liberally to 'dwell in Possibility' (Poem 657, c. 1862), an expression that is poetically indicative of inexhaustible 'possibilities' of connotation, rhetoricity and ellipsis, which are, in their turn, likely to generate an interminable repository of significations and explanations.

References

1. R. W. Littledale, *The Religious Education of Women* (London: Henry S. King & Co., 1874), pp. 33-4, in Lynda Palazzo, *Cristina Rossetti's Feminist Theology* (Basingstoke, Hampshire: Palgrave, 2002), p. 37.
2. Palazzo, *Cristina Rossetti's Feminist Theology*, p. 37.
3. *Ibid.*, p. 37.
4. *Ibid.*, p. 38.
5. *Ibid.*, p. 38.
6. Littledale, *The Religious Education of Women*, pp. 10-15, 25, 20, 33-34 in Palazzo, p. 37.
7. Palazzo, *Cristina Rossetti's Feminist Theology*, p. 37.
8. Quoted in Palazzo, p. 37.
9. Ruth Jenkins, *Reclaiming Myths of Power: Women Writers and the Victorian Spiritual Crisis* (Lewisburg: Bucknell University Press, 1995), p.26.
10. *Ibid.*, p. 26.
11. Palazzo, *Cristina Rossetti's Feminist Theology*, p. xiv.
12. Palazzo, *Cristina Rossetti's Feminist Theology*, p. xiv, quoting Florence Nightingale, Cassandra (New York: Westbury, 1979), p. 53.
13. Palazzo, Cristina Rossetti's Feminist Theology, p. xiv.
14. Jenkins, *Reclaiming Myths of Power*, p. 63.
15. Palazzo, *Cristina Rossetti's Feminist Theology*, p. xiv.
16. Mellisa Raphael, 'J. Ellice Hopkins: the Construction of a Recent Spiritual Feminist Foremother', in *Feminist Theology*, no. 13, September 1996, pp. 94, 93.

17. Palazzo, *Cristina Rossetti's Feminist Theology*, p. xiv.

18. Emily Dickinson, Poem 193, p. 139. All Emily-Dickinson Poems from 1 to 494 are taken from the following e-Source:*https://ia700301.us.archive.org/2/items/poemsofemilydick030097mbp/poemsofemilydick030097mbp.pdf*(Emily Dickinson, The Poems of Emily Dickinson, 3 vols. ed. Thomas H. Johnson [Cambridge, Massachusetts: Harvard University Press, 1955], Vol. 1 [Poems 1-494], Poem 312, p. 234.

19. Emily Dickinson, Poem 1487, All Emily-Dickinson Poems from 1 to 494 are taken from the following e-Source:*https://ia700301.us.archive.org/2/items/poemsofemilydick030097mbp/poemsofemilydick030097mbp.pdf*(Emily Dickinson, The Poems of Emily Dickinson, 3 vols. ed. Thomas H. Johnson [Cambridge, Massachusetts: Harvard University Press, 1955], Vol. 1 [Poems 1-494], Poem 312, p. 234.

20. *Ibid.*, Poem, 1543, c. 1882.

21. *Ibid.*, Poem 1735.

22. *Ibid.*, Poem 553.

23. *Ibid.*, Poem 527.

24. Emily Dickinson, *The Letters of (Le lettere di) Emily Dickinson – 331-360,* Letter to T. W. Higginson, No. 353, about October 1870. Source: *http://www.emilydickinson.it/l331-0360.html#notal0353*

25. Emily Dickinson, Poem 959(A loss of something ever felt I –).

26. Dorothy H. Oberhaus, *Emily Dickinson's Fascicles: Method and Meaning* (University Park: The Pennsylvania State University Press, 1995), p. 185.

27. *Ibid.*, p. 168.

28. Jane Donahue Eberwein, *Dickinson: Strategies of Limitation* (Amherst: The University of Massachusetts Press, 1985), p. 40.

29. Emily Dickinson, Poem 489.

30. Emily Dickinson, *Emily Dickinson: Selected Letters,* ed. Thomas H. Johnson (Cambridge, Massachusetts: Harvard University Press, 1958), No. 185, p. 136.

31. Emily Dickinson, Poem 623.
32. *Ibid.,* Poem 357, p. 284.
33. *Ibid.,* Poem 662.
34. *Ibid.,* Poem 827.
35. *Ibid.,* Poem 350, p.279.
36. *Ibid.,* Poem 836.
37. *Ibid.,* Poem 677.
38. *Ibid.,* Poem 751.
39. *Ibid.,* Poem 248, p. 179.
40. Stephen Cushman, *Fictions of Form in American Poetry* (Princeton, N. J.: Princeton University Press, 1993), p.50.
41. Emily Dickinson, *The Letters of Emily Dickinson,* 3 vols., eds. Thomas H. Johnson and Theodora Ward (Cambridge, Massachusetts: Harvard University Press, 1958), vol. 2, p. 408.

5

'The Morning after Death/ Is solemnest of industries': Voicing a Female Endurance of Death

> There's a certain slant of light,
> Winter Afternoons –
> That oppresses, like the Heft
> Of cathedral Tunes –[1]

Indeed, this 'certain slant of light' in 'Winter Afternoons' that oppresses like death, is a theme that we find to pervade Emily Dickinson's poetics. This idea of death is nevertheless intertwined with love, underneath of which run the sensibilities of despair and loss. Death, more often than not, follows from despondency and this significant perception is discernible in a handful of Dickinson's poems. In the above-mentioned poem, dejection is indubitably certain and inexorable. The expression 'heft' signifies weight with further associations of burden and anxiety. The cathedral tunes intimidate due to the grim oppression of faith, which they implore the listener to possess. Dickinson invests the poem with a dispassionate tone, as disengaged and nonchalant as the bleakest chronicle. The expression, 'There's a certain slant of light, / Winter Afternoons –', reveals a sense of desolation, bearing an unfamiliar association. It comprises the poet's artistic tropes which lead to the creation of a mysterious thought that emerging from the juxtaposition of apparently incongruous ideas. They subsequently give rise to a wholly weird array of significance conveying one unequivocal impression. The affiliation between 'a certain slant of light' and 'Winter Afternoons' may initially seem markedly inconsistent, but both the metaphors are actually made to form one single image of 'the Heft / Of Cathedral Tunes'. This act of metaphorization is therefore apparently almost vague, and yet immaculate. The epithet 'slant' offers us an inkling of a threatening logic and, hence, the neutrality and the seeming detachment of 'Winter Afternoons' appear to perplex us with a sinister enticement emerging from the oppressive echoes of the metaphor of 'Cathedral Tunes'. At the beginning of the second stanza, this 'slant of light' inflicts 'Heavenly Hurt', thereby giving rise to a difference within, 'Where the meanings are now?' What emerges out from this ostensible distinction in the incongruously employed imagery is the manifestation of nature, which is as atypical and inexplicable as the cathedral tunes, and an inalienable music, that is both devouring and beatific. Taking these metaphors together, Dickinson feels the oppressive 'heft' and in anguish and resignation depicts, 'An imperial affliction / Sent us of the air'. This 'affliction' casts a significant dominance over the landscape:

> When it comes, the Landscape listens –
> Shadows – hold their breath –
> When it goes, 'tis like the Distance
> On the look of Death –

Here, we feel a certain similitude between the poet's situation and that of the 'Landscape', both experiencing the consternation. The 'slant of light' appears as being ominous and shares a hostile relationship with nature. Though there is a situational affinity between the poet and the landscape, there develops a distance between them. When the latter is tormented by dejection, which is revealed in the form of 'Shadows' holding 'their breath', the poet envisions a distant death, that eventually signifies the ultimate form of reality. Distance has a close association with death in many of Dickinson's poems, particularly in her love poems, in which the non-existence of the lover is intensely felt as death. The dejection here is associated with death and is metaphorized as a 'seal' which, in its turn, symbolizes the truth of mortality that man is inevitably subject to. It is this seal that lends the poem a sense of finality as it draws towards the close.

Death is, hence, seen to approach with utter hopelessness and the close association that the two share is prominent in the following poem:

> The difference between Despair
> And fear – is like the One
> Between the instant of a Wreck –
> And when the Wreck has been –[2]

The above delineation offers a brusque description of the discrepancy that exists between 'despair' and 'fear', the former being associated with the moment of annihilation and the latter with the aftermath of such destruction. Despair is also associated with motionlessness and tranquillity of the 'Eye / Upon the Forehand of a Bust':

> The Mind is smooth – no Motion –
> Contented as the Eye
> Upon the Forehead of a Bust
> That knows – it cannot see –[3]

The poet feels content with the eyes made frozen by death. The stroke of death could not take away the placidity of her mind. The poet's heart finds solace and reassurance in the realization of its trans-temporal state of existence. In yet another poem, she unravels the ecstasy she experienced, 'A perfect-paralyzing Bliss', unconditional and consummate. For Dickinson, content and despair are analogous in the sense that both the sensations are not only inalienable and commensurate, but are also immaculate. One of the remarkable characteristics of Dickinsonian poetics is that, she lends an equal form of completeness and purity to both pain and bliss. To her, both are plausible and fundamental and hence, elated and felicitous.

Emily Dickinson's creativity entailed an essential constituent of gradual undoing, since she believed that both love and poetry are associated with visions of God and eventually lead to death. Death, in its turn, is so perfectly inevitable that it stands as being relentlessly conclusive. To Dickinson, 'To be alive – is Power',[4] since death usurps all the vitality of life revealing the fact that, it is not merely apocalyptic, but also indicates the sense of extinction of all forms of life.

As a woman writer, Dickinson perceives with a sense of anguish that, 'I made my soul familiar – with her extremity – / That at the last, it should not be a novel "Agony"'. She engages herself in the act of familiarization with the most perfect form of reality or, in the poet's word, life's 'extremity' to take on the agony that death is perceived to carry with it. It seems that the poet feels death within her and wishes the soul to be 'acquainted – / Meet tranquillity, as friends' so much so that life becomes a tranquil experience. In 'The last night that She lived',[5] Dickinson registers that, 'It was a Common Night / Except the Dying – this tolls / Made Nature different'. The bemoaners are aware of all occurrences and nondescript entities are 'Italicized – as 'twere'. The impressions are rather quotidian here:

> We waited while She passed –
> It was a narrow time –
> Too jostled were Our Souls to speak
> At length the notice came.

The bewailers only look on when the departed retires. This postponement is repressive and hence the time constricting. During the spell that prefaced death, the acquaintances are well shown as appearing for the funeral, resting around the corpse and assembling together. The language in Emily Dickinson's poems on death can perhaps be represented with no greater precision and profundity than the following:

> The language of soul is taken from the language of body, as the language of eternity is derived from the language of time, because there is no other language. All language is, in this sense, domestic. Death poems are life poems.[6]

Dickinson's poems on the theme of death bear testimony to the above position and it is this insight that lends them their unprecedented literary strength. She has combined the subliminal essence of language with the metaphor of domesticity to pen some of the greatest poems in the language. 'Too jostled were Our Souls to speak' since the poet strives staggeringly with her art to express her experiences and enrobe them with language. 'Jostled' is emblematic of a thespian urge mingled with an implication of the idea of domesticity, making another certainty very clear that what is trans-experiential has to either acknowledge a 'finite language'[7] or remain silent. As the poem concludes, the grievers feel reassured to go back to their lives: 'And then an awful leisure was / Belief to regulate', and to usher in 'a discipline domestic in its language, esoteric in its particular application'.[8] The repertory of words that Dickinson uses in her poetry is greatly dependent on the metaphor of domesticity, which is expressed with such grace that her poetry becomes a novel art, particularly because the expressions she employs do not associate semantically with such domestic commonality. Hence, her sense of rapture, that marks the poems as quintessentially Dickinsonian, usually offers a fallacious impression, though later it is perceived to be unobtrusively true:

> I died for Beauty – but was scarce
> Adjusted in the Tomb[9]

Perhaps, the magnificence of Dickinson's verse lies in the fact that she deploys an apparently nondescript language with such skill that her authorial craftsmanship can seldom be disputed. The convergence of subtle ideas and a seemingly unpretentious language leads to the formation of a heightened form of creation:

> I heard a Fly buzz – when I died –
> The Stillness in the Room
> Was like the Stillness in the Air –
> Between the Heaves of Storm –[10]

This prologue to Poem 465 demonstrates that the speaker speaks after her death, an occasion when she could sense the tranquil ambience of the 'Room' to be in consonance with the unstirring peacefulness of the 'Air'. The mourners have gathered around and the metaphors of 'Eyes' and 'Breaths' usher in a kind of a backdrop representative of a deathbed scene:

> The Eyes around – had wrung them dry –
> And Breaths were gathering firm
> For that last Onset – when the King
> Be witnessed – in the Room –

Such a doleful episode is 'interposed' by 'a Fly' with 'Blue – uncertain stumbling Buzz / Between the light – and me – / And then the Windows failed – and then / I could not see to see –.' Death alienates the speaker from life, represented primarily by the 'Eyes' and 'Breaths' and more significantly by the 'Fly' with its 'stumbling Buzz'. 'That last Onset' (the word conspicuous by a whimsical yet a connotative Dickinsonian upper case) was corroborated by the fact that 'the Windows failed – and then / I could not see to see –.' The poet feels anxious and distraught by the 'blueness' and uncertainty of the finality of her being and she could feel life, being on the threshold of death, from the stirrings of the emblematic fly. This onslaught obscures her vision and she is eventually distanced from the 'light' of creativity by the fly, the inspiring Muse, whizzing past the 'Windows' and shutting her from the outside world, that is much opposed to her wish and desire. The sense of alienation from the world of human existence creates in the poet a consciousness of futility and nothingness. This act of 'nihilization' gives birth to a feeling of numbness in her ability of self-definition through poetry is concerned.

Another remarkable instance of Dickinsonian theorization of death is Poem 712 (1862), where the poet delineates her own conceptual world, familiarizing the ultimate truth of mortality with the commonality of the domestic truth of survival. The poet conjures up a stage, whereupon the actors play their parts:

> Because I could not stop for Death –
> He kindly stopped for me –

The Carriage held but just Ourselves –
And Immortality.

It is true that while 'Yeats speaks of "that discourtesy of death", Emily Dickinson enacts its civility.'[11] We find an entirely different portrayal of death in this poem to what we found in 'I heard a Fly buzz'. The patrician here comes down and accompanies the lady to the 'Carriage'. The poem brings us close to the reminiscences of Robert Browning's 'The Last Ride Together', with which it has been compared:

What if we still ride on, we too
With life forever old yet new,
Changed not in kind but in degree,
The instant made eternity ...

Not only did Emily Dickinson read the poem with care, but was also moved by a line in the second stanza, 'So one day more am I deified'. However, she departed from the notion of deification of the self, which together with the other, has come to constitute, for her, the 'me'. In Dickinson, 'we' comprises the self, and Death, the other. The speaker observes all the happenings of the phenomenal world and 'slowly' drives towards 'Eternity' accompanied by remarkable 'Civility'. She virtually succumbs to the gentleman in the 'Carriage', but her experience of life is barely melancholic. She does not fail to recognize the 'School, where Children strove / at Recess – in the Ring –', 'the Fields of Gazing Grain –', 'the Setting Sun –', each of which is nonetheless important to the speaker's perception of life. The reader feels somewhat struck by the conjectural antithesis she puts forward in the terminal stanza:

Since then – 'tis Centuries – and yet
Feels shorter than the Day
I first surmised the Horses' Heads
Were toward Eternity –

The verse here perhaps lays itself bare to our presupposition that the poet-speaker reconciles herself to 'Eternity' without any protest, but she does yearn for those apparently insignificant temporal events, which provide her with the essential constituent elements for her poetry. In a later poem that can be brought into context as an analogous text here is Poem 1445, where Dickinson personifies death as 'the supple Suitor / That wins at last.' Both the poems portray death with an overtone of care and tenderness. In this poem, the progress towards death is demonstrated not as a ride towards immortality, but as 'a stealthy wooing / Conducted first / By pallid innuendoes / And din approach'. The essence of these lines of verse differs from that of the former poem in that it brings forth a different portrayal of death, from which we feel a magnificent theme to be at work. The grandeur and flamboyance of 'Because I could not stop for Death' lies in the dignified, solemn and slow drive across the outstretched vista of the countryside and the courteous gentleman 'paused before a House', which was almost in ruins, to enable the driven to catch a glimpse of the threatened existence of the derelict construction. Hence, the conclusion is characterized by a contemplative aftermath sans the sonorous 'Bugles'. The juxtaposition of two strikingly assorted images of death, the act of kindly stopping for the poet-speaker so that 'The Carriage held but just Ourselves' on the one hand, and on the other, that of stealthily wooing primarily by 'pallid innuendoes', braving 'at last with Bugles' and bearing away 'in triumph / To Troth unknown', evokes a distinctive array of multifarious modes of signification that perhaps confounds the poet herself and causes her to struggle to convey the uncertainty of this finality, that stealthily approaches, but surely destroys.

We do, of course, perceive the elegance of Dickinson's verse that lies in its ability to thrive upon so commonplace domestic ingredients. It seems she conceptualizes her own universe of thoughts, which considerably draws upon the apparently mundane experiences, and through an extraordinary act of poetic creation subsequently transcends them to form a trans-temporal reality. This unique element of calm self-confidence in the poetic persona is discernible in another poem:

The Bustle in a House
The Morning after Death
Is solemnest of industries
Enacted upon Earth – [12]

Thus death, for Dickinson here, comes as a lover and Albert J. Gelpi appositely puts it in the following way:

> ... since death was crowned with power, he came as a lover-king; since death justified the "Guilt" of love, he came as a lover-redeemer. Dying itself was merely the passage, often depicted as a carriage ride, to love, coronation, heaven.[13]

We find one instance of this idea in the inaugural stanza of 'Because I could not stop for Death'. Here, another poem (Poem 1123) comes into context which speaks of the 'tender Carpenter' nailing the coffin down implying death of the lover on the one hand, and the metaphor of the 'sovereign Carpenter' or Christ who is indicative of death, on the other. This act of metaphorization might not be very consciously achieved by the poet but such a purport is almost effortlessly expected, considering the magnificence of linguistic workmanship evident in Dickinson's verse. Hence, we find in her poetry a significant plethora of images of death, where she refers to death as 'democratic': 'The Beggar and his Queen / Propitiate this Democrat.' This description of death as a 'Democrat' along with the fact that, 'Death's large – Democratic fingers / Rub away the Brand' of 'Color – Caste – Denomination –', did not seem adequate to her, since the idea of death could not merely be implicated with the notion of an enigmatic equalizer and destroyer. She does not also ignore the fact that death's imperial sovereignty accords 'One dignity' to all the subjects, each one of whom is not dispossessed of the enormous prerogative owned by her or him. Thus it can justly be maintained that, '... the brides of death were democrat-queens; the kingdom of death was an egalitarian Empire of Czars as small as Everyman.'[14] The identification of the poetic self with death appears to be overwhelmingly consummate on the one hand, and on the other, to reflect the uncertainty and unforeseeability of the royal 'Redeemer' as well as the accompanying doubt that tears apart the poetic mind which, in its turn, envisages the process of transmutation of life thus:

> Where, then, does love become life? Only after the pain – 'over there'. 'Till Death – is narrow Loving –' but then 'Love is immortality.' No wonder that immortality is 'the Flood subject'. When she and the lover had bound each other to the cross, the figure of the man blurred with that of Christ, and as she shared in the exquisite agony of His love, so she would share in His resurrection as well. Out of danger in the Eden-Heaven, all the emotional and religious frustrations which she had endured at such expense would be lost in her fulfilment in and absorption by the 'lover'; for 'years of troth have taught thee / More than Wifehood ever may!' Sometimes heaven ('Old Suitor Heaven') meant an eternity wed to God, the 'distant-stately Lover'. Then she would be 'Bride of the Father and the Son / Bride of the Holy Ghost': 'What omnipotence lies in wait / For her to be a Bride'. Sometimes Jesus was, explicitly or implicitly, the courtly gentleman, the Redeemer who became her Master; at other times she rejected Jesus for her 'lover' and looked forward to an immortality of 'you and me' in Paradise. The identity of the heavenly 'lover' – God, man, or God-man – was often indeterminate, a shape projected by the need of the isolate self.[15]

Death may be ambivalent, unpredictable, cryptic and speculative, but love, for Dickinson, is certain, invariable, and unwavering. It is this momentum that invigorates life, transcends the spatio-temporal sense of death and brings about resurrection. To put in her own words, it is 'anterior to Life – / Posterior to Death'.[16] It is a journey towards immortality, where the throes of love find fulfilment 'in ravished Holiness' accompanied by an excruciating 'Anger grander than Delight' as well as a riotous 'Transport wild as thrills the Graves'. Dickinson here is perplexed by her own anxiety of authorship. She expresses her disquietude by saying, 'I cannot live with You – … I could not die – with You – … Nor could I rise – with You –', the experience ultimately leading to despondency and eventual resignation: 'that White

Sustenance – / Despair'.[17] The idea of immortality is almost everywhere in Dickinson's poetry and the juxtaposition of the apparently irreconcilable thoughts of hope and despair is astonishing. The poet even associated immortality with consciousness and with flashes of subtle insight. She contemplated immortality as the only inevitable phenomenon, bearing a profound significance as love and death, and revealing for her 'an existential state of mind and feeling'.[18] It is the consciousness, an inseparable human faculty, that enables the poet to experience such a beatific and 'deathless' moment. She could experience love in its agony, death in its destruction and immortality in its unique palpability, through her secluded poetic self.

Dickinson was gifted with an amazing sense of artistry to imbibe and transform the Romantic convention of deployment of language into such a form of linguistic usage that unfolds 'the identity of the exclusive self'.[19] There is a complete identification of the poetic self with the sepulchre, particularly due to the essence of solitude the latter bears; nature now can barely be understood to exist outside the poet, who herself becomes the very objects she experiences and writes about:

> The setting is understood to contain the writer in the act of writing: the poet in the grip of what he feels and sees, and primitively inspired to carve it in the living rock.[20]

The setting for Dickinson is truly the poetic self that has itself transformed, through the act of writing, into a 'living rock' upon which are epigraphed a multitude of experiences of love and affliction:

> I've dropped my Brain – My Soul is numb –
> The Veins that used to run
> Stop palsied – 'tis Paralysis
> Done perfecter on stone.[21]

This metaphor of 'Paralysis', and the palsied 'Veins that used to run' are all engraved 'perfecter' on the stone of the self. In *Emily Dickinson's Poetry: Stairway*, Charles R. Anderson examines Poem

341, 'After great pain, a formal feeling comes', and he explores the 'symbols of crystallization' and the essence of the stone as conceived by Dickinson:

> As the images of a funeral rite subside, two related ones emerge to body forth the victim who is at once a living organism and a frozen form. Both are symbols of crystallization: "Freezing" in the snow, which is neither life nor death but both simultaneously; and 'A Quartz contentment like a stone', for the paradoxical serenity that follows intense suffering. This recalls her envy of the 'little Stone', happy because unconscious of the exigencies that afflict mortals, and points forward to the paradox in another poem, 'Contended as despair'. Such is the 'formal feeling' that comes after great pain. It is, ironically no feeling at all, only numb rigidness existing outside time and space.[22]

Another instance shows Dickinson transforming from a living and throbbing being into a lifeless fragment of marble:

> Vitality is Carved and cool
> My nerve in Marble lies –
> A breathing Woman
> Yesterday – Endowed with Paradise.

She, being now 'Endowed with Paradise', toils hard to retrieve herself from this transfiguration in the expectation of going back to her earlier state of life, when her actions were not fettered by the catastrophic power of such fatality:

> Who wrought Carrara in me
> And chiselled all my tune
> Were it a witchcraft – were it death –
> I've still a chance to strain
>
> To Being somewhere – Motion – Breath
> Though Centuries beyond,
> And every limit a decade –
> I'll shiver, satisfied.[23]

Through this yearning of the soul, echoes the Christian belief of resurrection. Dickinson has endorsed the most intense expressions of the barrow to demonstrate her inexplicable predicament. Subtle as Dickinson's strokes of significance are, she goes to the extent of imparting emotional implications to her verse. The unidentified 'Who' wrought a blotch in her and 'chiselled' all her 'time', an act that causes a numbness in her sensations requiring her to strive for centuries to resuscitate her tortured self, and a sense of agitation causing her to ruminate. The poet's consternation is nevertheless perceptible in many of her poems in which we can also trace an experience of agony and soreness, engraved on the marble of her consciousness.

This image of a perfect art on the stone of the self does not, however, necessarily pivot on the affliction threatened by an anonymous 'who'. Dickinson envisages the circumstance after death in one of her early poems of 1860:

> If I shouldn't be alive
> When the Robins come,
> Give the one in Red Cravat
> A memorial crumb.
>
> If I couldn't thank you,
> Being fast asleep,
> You will know I'm trying
> With my Granite lip![24]

The poet feels the granite within her and the stone precluded her from communicating with the living. She goes on straining herself to express her thoughts on the one hand, and on the other, gives in the competence of the breathing self of the other. What agonizes the female poet here is the oppression she feels of not being able to articulate her experience of the world. She would find herself greatly relieved if the pulsating other can perform the generous task of apportioning a 'memorial crumb' to the Robin, an act that will, by its virtue, perpetuate the poet's elevated task. The poet here becomes the stone and yet endeavours infinitely to struggle against the forced silence that her 'Granite lip' has disagreeably cast her into. Joanne Feit Diehl correctly points out in *Dickinson and the Romantic Imagination*:

> The granite lip, rendered incapable of speech, is controlled by a "will" which supersedes the body's capacity to respond – effort outlasts mortality. The struggle of the granite lip to speak after death acknowledges the effort of the vital being as it confronts the pressures that urge her into silence; hence the need of another voice, the voice of the reader, who wins the poet's stifled thanks for carrying out the generous task of giving a crumb to a bird, the "memorial crumb" which keeps the poet's memory alive.[25]

This identification of the self with the stone, resulting in a 'psychic numbing', metaphorically finds expression in the poem, 'After great pain, a formal feeling comes –', with an overwhelming sense of stupefaction:

> After great pain, a formal feeling comes –
> The Nerves sit ceremonious, like Tombs –
> The stiff Heart, questions was it He, that bore,
> And Yesterday, or Centuries before?

Death brings to the poet an unnerving sensation and this psychic numbness has cast her into an eternal oblivion. Here again, she self metamorphoses into stone. The poet talks of benumbing senses by indicating specifically the physical positions of the nerves, heart and the feet:

> The Feet, mechanical, go round –
> Of ground, or Air, or Ought –
> A Wooden way
> Regardless grown,
> A Quartz contentment, like a stone –

The self provides the background to the poem and is itself marked by a stark inanity and emptiness. The direction of movement remains unknown to the inane self, stumbling as on 'A Wooden way', yet 'Regardless', and betraying 'A Quartz contentment', itself being transformed into a stone:

> This is the Hour of Lead –
> Remembered, if outlived,

As Freezing persons, recollect the Snow –
First – Chill – then Stupor – then the letting go –

The self gradually sails from consciousness to 'Stupor' and the transition is 'the Hour of Lead', the hour of slipping into unconsciousness beyond all spatio-temporal materiality of human existence. The entire saga of life ultimately consists of this peregrination to death, that ushers in 'a formal feeling' and a 'Quartz contentment'. The irony intended by the epithet 'quartz' can barely be overlooked. The inherent malaise and anxiety seems very evident and the poet is apprehensive about confronting 'the Hour of Lead'. Oblivion prevents her creativity and the cessation, that death causes to her thought, is perhaps the eternal 'letting go' of her poetic faculty to communicate to the world of the living.

Emily Dickinson, as correctly traced by Elizabeth Phillips in *Emily Dickinson: Personae and Performance*,[26] had been familiar with the death of Amherst women from the days of her childhood. It was perhaps, as Phillips presumes, the death of her Boston aunt, Lavinia Norcross, the mother of Emily's cousins Louise and Frances (then eighteen and twelve respectively) on April 17, 1860, that forms the emotional essence of the poem. Lavinia married her cousin Loring Norcross against the wishes of the family and happened to be the poet's favourite aunt. The poet recorded in February 1859: 'My mother's only sister has had an invalid winter, and Vinnie has gone to enliven the house, and make the days shorter for my sick aunt.'[27] Dickinson again refers to her aunt in a letter in September:

> Mother's favourite sister is sick, and mother will have to bid her good-night .... the aunt whom Vinnie visits .... Does God take care of those at sea? My aunt is such a timid woman![28]

Coming to know about the death of aunt Lavinia, Dickinson exclaims in sorrow and desolation:

> Blessed Aunt Lavinia now; all the world goes out, and I see nothing but her room, and angels bearing her into those great countries in the blue sky of which we don't know anything .... Well, she is safer now

> than 'we know or even think.' Tired little aunt, sleeping ne'er so peaceful![29]

The poet staggers while she endeavours to give expression to her untold woe and remorse. She sheds tears in unbearable affliction and misery. She reminisces in agony about 'how still' Aunt Lavinia rested 'while I was making the little loaf and fastening ... flowers'[30] to send them to her. She was overwhelmed with unrestrained grief when she wrote:

> Oh! Vinnie, it is dark and strange to think of summer afterward! How she loved the summer! The birds keep singing just the same. Oh! The thoughtless birds![31]

Another poem that bemoans the death of the poet's most preferred aunt is, 'How many times these low feet staggered'.[32] The poem conveys a sense of Gothic gruesomeness and trepidation:

> How many times these low feet staggered –
> Only the soldered mouth can tell –
> Try – can you stir the awful rivet –
> Try – can you lift the hasps of steel!
>
> ....
>
> Fearless – the cobweb swings from the ceiling –
> Indolent Housewife – in Daisies – lain!

It seems that the poet caresses her aunt and the poem, with all certainty, expresses the concern and emotional fervour that she attached to her aunt, due to whose absence the house now wears a dilapidated look. The 'dull flies', 'the freckled pane' and the 'fearless' 'cobweb' are all surely emblematic of the horrifying absence of Lavinia Dickinson. The poet magnifies the character and employs the metaphor of the 'Indolent Housewife', who has long been enduring severe illness and now is laid in an unostentatious bunch of daisies. Dickinson is grief-stricken and through delineating the derelict house, contemplates her aunt's death, since we can seldom doubt the implication that underpins the idea of 'Indolent Housewife'. Death, here, is a motif which the poet does not resort to as a solace and reassurance, but rather as a benumbing reality, the extreme disappointment of which can only be forgotten by the death of the physical self, which eventually makes it possible for her to detach herself from all consciousness of the temporal world. For Dickinson, the pragmatist, 'Drama's Vitallest Expression is the Common Day / That arise and set about Us',[33] and this drama of life and afterlife is always 'infinite enacted' 'In the Human Heart' with unique perpetuity.

Death, seen in its myriad perspectives, brings Dickinson to describe herself as a corpse in one of her verses, and hence this has provoked a critic to consider the representation as one of Dickinson's 'most obviously hostile autobiographical poems'.[34] This poem exhibits a transformation of the subject, who envisages her own death as having 'the charm of a genre painting', and illustrates the fact that 'a change of voice is a change of style' for her:

> 'Twas just this time, Last year. I died.
> I know I heard the Corn,
> When I was Carried by the Farms –
> It had the Tassels on –

The poet lamented for being deprived of the 'Christmas glee', and the 'drama' of the 'common day' torments her since she plays a character who does not take part in the immense mirth of the Thanks giving celebration:

> I wondered which would miss me, least,
> And when Thanksgiving, came.
> If Father'd multiply the plates –
> To make an Even Sum –[35]

The nostalgia, the pain of a relational familiarity and the sense of lack, emerging from the inability to associate the physically dead self with the temporality of the earthly happenings, cause an overwhelming melancholy in the omniscient poet-narrator. She clings on to the reminiscences as a source of consolation for her reclusivity and passionately craves to go back to the moment she once cherished. The poet wishes to script the never-ending 'theatre' of life and she records it in her immortal verses. Her life is undesirably put an end to by an unsolicited and immature death which becomes the cause of her angst, since she is forced to take an objective stance that impairs expression and necessitates insufferable silence and passivity.

As we examine the authorial intention in the poems, 'How many times these low feet staggered –' and "Twas just this time, last year, I died', the latter dated two years after, we find that the poet is quick enough to take a trans-thematic leap from individual emotions and sensibilities, which are often confused and nebulous, to a kind of poetry, dispossessed of the cares and obligations of the self.

A writer, who has over 1700 poems to her credit and 1000 known letters, is seldom voiceless. Instead, Dickinson appears to condemn silence, not only because she endorses the supremacy of words, but since she is rather prone to be even more sceptical about the effectiveness of silence. She is a poet who scarcely glorifies silence and begins a poem with 'Silence is all we dread':

> There's ransom in a Voice –
> But Silence is Infinity.
> Himself have not a voice.[36]

What Dickinson was anxious about was the way in which she would make silence 'a part of the linguistic experience'[37]:

> There is no Silence in the Earth – so silent.
> As that endured
> Which uttered, would discourage Nature
> And haunt the World.[38]

Silence, for Dickinson, may be discouraging since it implies an event of ghastly death that appals and intimidates. It may denote an utter disengagement rather than a rapturous union. E. Miller Budick describes it as 'the lonesome, eternal distance created by a "ransom" or a redemption that dangles unattainably beyond humankind's reach.'[39] The consternation of the poet arises from the fact that it is language that can contort meaning, and silence thus signifies the 'absence of meaning, the ultimate cosmic default',[40] creating a void that renders all poetic expression impossible. Hence, in poem 1296, Dickinson says:

> Death's Waylaying not the sharpest
> Of the thefts of Time –
> There Marauds a sorer Robber,
> Silence – is his name –
> No Assault, nor any Menace
> Doth betoken him.
> But from Life's consummate Cluster –
> He supplants the Balm.

The poet is clearly apprehensive of the threatening marauder called 'Silence', that 'supplants' not only 'Life's consummate Cluster', but is itself more perilous than 'Death's Waylaying'. Thus silence can even unsettle meanings and cause them to cease, not to talk of conveying significances that 'lie magically beyond human verbalization.'[41] As Dickinson implies in another poem:

> Great Streets of silence led away.
> To Neighborhoods of Pause –
> Here was no Notice – no Dissent
> No Universe – no Laws[42]

We find here that silence obliterates all laws of the Universe leading only to an eternal and devastating 'Pause'. It has rendered all earthly time as well as language meaningless. Language fails to generate meaning and hence renders the poet incapable of expression. Thus silence accompanies death, a reality that utterly separates a dead person from all forms of breathing life. The distance is unending and unbridgeable. Only some sore impressions like, 'little Workmanships / In Crayon, or in Wool', 'the thimble', 'the stitches', 'A Book' and the exiguous pencil 'Etchings',[43] remain. These are seemingly insignificant objects on which the poet thrives, with the help of which she creates and from which she derives her expression. Hence, death and silence may rob off the poet's precious acquaintances, but not her power of self-expression.

References

1. All Emily-Dickinson Poems from 1 to 494 are taken from the following e-Source: *https://ia700301.us.archive.org/2/items/poemsofemilydick030097mbp/poemsofemilydick030097mbp.pdf* (Emily Dickinson, The Poems of Emily Dickinson, 3 vols. ed. Thomas H. Johnson [Cambridge, Massachusetts: Harvard University Press, 1955], Vol. 1 [Poems 1-494], Poem 258, p. 185.
2. Emily Dickinson, Poem 305, p. 226.
3. *Ibid.*, Poem 305, p. 227.
4. *Ibid.*, Poem 677.
5. *Ibid.*, Poem 1100.
6. Leonard Unger ed.-in-chief, *American Writers: A Collection of Literary Biographies* (University of Minnesota: Charles Scribner's Sons, 1974), p. 467.
7. *Ibid.*, p. 467.
8. *Ibid.*, p. 467.
9. Emily Dickinson, Poem 449, p. 347.
10. *Ibid.*, Poem 465, p. 358.
11. Unger, *American Writers*, p. 468.
12. Emily Dickinson, Poem 1078. All Emily-Dickinson Poems from 495 to 1775 are taken from the following e-Source: *http://archive.csustan.edu/english/reuben/pal/chap4/dickinson.html* (Thomas H. Johnson ed. *Complete Poems* [Boston: Little, Brown & Co., 1960], as a part of PAL: Perspectives in American Literature – A Research and Reference Guide, An Ongoing Online Project, Paul P. Reuben [copyright]).
13. Albert J. Gelpi, *Emily Dickinson: The Mind of the Poet* (Cambridge, Massachusetts: Harvard University Press, 1965), p. 113.
14. *Ibid.*, p. 113.
15. *Ibid.*, p. 114.
16. Emily Dickinson, Poem 917.

17. Emily Dickinson, Poem 640.
18. Gelpi, *Emily Dickinson: The Mind of the Poet*, p. 115.
19. Joanne Feit Diehl, *Dickinson and the Romantic Imagination* (Princeton, N. J.: Princeton University Press, 1981), p. 45.
20. Geoffrey Hartman, 'Wordsworth, Inscriptions, and Romantic Nature Poetry', in eds. Frederick W. Hilles and Harold Bloom, *From Sensibility to Romanticism* (New York: Oxford University Press, 1965), p. 400.
21. Emily Dickinson, Poem 1046.
22. Charles R. Anderson, *Emily Dickinson's Poetry: Stairway* (New York: Holt, Rinehart and Winston, 1960), p. 211.
23. Emily Dickinson, Poem 1046.
24. *Ibid.*, Poem 182, p. 133.
25. Diehl, *Dickinson and the Romantic Imagination*, p. 47.
26. Elizabeth Phillips, *Emily Dickinson: Personae and Performance* (University Park and London: The Pennsylvania State University Press, 1988), p. 90.
27. Emily Dickinson, *The Letters of Emily Dickinson*, 3 vols. eds. Thomas H. Johnson and Theodora Ward, (Cambridge, Massachusetts: Harvard University Press, 1958), vol. 2, p. 346.
28. *Ibid.*, vol. 2, p. 354.
29. *Ibid.*, vol. 2, pp. 361-62.
30. *Ibid.*, vol. 2, pp. 361-62.
31. *Ibid.*, vol. 2, pp. 361-62.
32. Emily Dickinson, Poem 187, pp. 135-36.
33. *Ibid.*, Poem 741.
34. Vivian R. Pollak, *Dickinson. The Anxiety of Gender* (Ithaca and London: Cornell University Press, 1984), p. 55.
35. Emily Dickinson, Poem 445.
36. *Ibid.*, Poem 1251.
37. E. Miller Budick, *Emily Dickinson and the Life of Language: A Study in Symbolist Poetics* (Baton Rouge: Louisiana State University Press, 1985), p. 165.

38. Emily Dickinson, Poem 1004.

39. Budick, *Emily Dickinson and the Life of Language: A Study in Symbolist Poetics*, p. 165.

40. *Ibid.*, p. 165.

41. *Ibid.*, p. 165.

42. Emily Dickinson, Poem 1159.

43. *Ibid.*, Poem 360, pp. 286-87.

Conclusion

'Wherefore, My Baffled Fingers, / Thy Perplexity?': The Woman Writer and the Anxiety of Secluded Female Art

> [The] girl or woman … tries to write because she is peculiarly susceptible to language. She goes to poetry or fiction looking for *her* way of being in the world, since she too has been putting words and images together; she is looking eagerly for guides, maps, possibilities; and over and over again in the words' 'masculine persuasive force' of literature she comes up against something that negates everything she is about: she meets the image of Woman in books written by men. She finds a terror and a dream, she finds a beautiful pale face, she finds Juliet or Tess or Salome, but precisely what she does not find is that absorbed, drudging, puzzled, sometimes inspired creature, herself, who sits at a desk trying to put words together.[1]

The 'image of Woman' as conceived by the male poet 'negates everything she is about', since the preoccupation of writing does not perfectly accord with her experience, and moreover, such creations have their presupposedly unexceptional implications of impassive quiescence detrimental to creativity.

An illustrious saga of the agony and anguish of female creativity informs Sandra Gilbert and Susan Gubar's epoch-making review of women writers, *The Madwoman in the Attic: The Woman Writer and the Nineteenth Century Literary Imagination* (1979). The authority of women's literary imagination within the domain of an inhibiting patriarchal prerogative is what the study registers.

The dilemma arising out of an authoritarian convention is symbolized at the very beginning by presenting a narrative of Snow White, in which the Wicked Queen is transformed into an ill-fated feminist exemplar, revolting against the tortures of the patriarchal king who remains predominantly concealed. Here, the queen is emblematic of a diverse array of poets and novelists. The significance of the story lies in revealing the harsh reality of the life of the woman writer being torn by the internal contradiction between her role of an ideal daughter of patriarchy and her right to write. The experience of the woman writer is encapsulated in the chronicle of how the Queen, 'a plotter, an artist, an impersonator, a woman of almost infinite creative energy, witty, wily and self-absorbed as artists traditionally are',[2] endeavours to exterminate her phlegmatic, yet graceful, antagonist by 'the traditionally female arts of tight lacing, cosmetology and cuisine, but her three "plots" succeed only in transforming her rival into the eternally beautiful, intimate object d' art preserved in the glass coffin of patriarchal aesthetics';[3] 'the artist ending up by doing the death-dance in red-hot shoes, condemned under patriarchy to monstrosity and self-destruction.'[4]

Through bringing this anecdote of the woman writer and her struggle against the stringent compartmentalization of her traditionally prescribed social role into context, the authors assert on the necessity of the artist to give unhindered expression to her self-definition:

> Before women can even attempt that pen which is so rigorously kept from them, they must escape just those male texts which, defining them as "Cyphers", deny them the authority to formulate alternatives to an authority which has imprisoned them and kept them from attempting the pen.[5]

The wish of the creator is to 'dance out of the looking-glass of the male text into a tradition that enabled her to create her own authority'.[6] The thesis of the book thus comprises the experiences of 'hunger, rebellion and rage'[7] in paradigmatic works by female authors.

In her initial literary sensitivity, we recognize Emily Dickinson dithering between two stark and inapposite artistic positions, one of them being precluded by the obligation of performance and self-definition and the other being impeded by gender. This is the dilemma which she experienced when she tried to find a situation where the woman writer could establish herself irreconcilably and in which she would not merely fantasize, but articulate.

This predicament of women writers was perhaps due to the fact that female creativity is hardly able to transcend the individual and the perfunctory. A majority of women were deficient in classical indoctrination that formed the basis for introduction into 'high' culture. Conventional constructs on the function of a poet, for example, were immanently virile. Publication was considered to be a presumptuous and unfeminine self-exposure, or even overt self-ostentation, which became more conveniently legitimized when one composed novels in order to amass money and seldom wrote poems that brought only fame. Novel writing was a preoccupation that was more comfortable for women primarily because of its less intimidating masculine convention, even though it involved less regard. It is often so conceived that it was more challenging for women to evoke the consciousness of the self and self-affirmation that poetry demands and that they were too inhibited to write assertive and enthusiastic verse.[8] The acclaimed nineteenth-century critic, R. H. Hutton, maintains that female imagination is not able to unfasten itself from 'the visible surface and form of human existence'.[9] It was thus problematical for women to position themselves within the rubric of the legacy of English poetry that, in its turn, corroborated the intellectual and subjective restrictions.

The contemporary critics woman writer was necessitated by such an overwhelmingly male literary tradition to situate herself in two positions. Her predicament appears to have its origin in the certainty that considered writing poetry as a womanly activity, in spite of the fact that men were presumed to do it. Critics preferred poetic compositions with unpretentious and ingenuous expressions inspired by artless and instinctive sensations which are customarily believed to be more idiosyncratic of women.

The mélange of poetry and femininity, surprisingly enough, proscribed female poets. Women were thus rather objects of art than creators of such art. It was the formidable male poets who gave expression to their creative personae through illustrious female figures, for instance, Tennyson's Mariana and Lady of Shalott, Browning's Pippa and Balaustion and Arnold's Iseult of Brittany, representing only a part of the poet's self and his artistic consciousness, that is conceived as being cloistered from and unacquainted with the external world and the extensive spectrum of human knowledge and experience. Such representative figures could seldom produce art themselves. Their creators performed this imaginative task for them. Hence, a woman writer who juxtaposed herself with such a form of impassioned and secluded art would rather seldom, than occasionally, be accomplished enough to write.

Emily Dickinson, who is indubitably the most outstanding woman poet of the English language, certainly requires to be considered from the historical, subliminal, cultural and artistic standpoints of her femininity. The fundamental premise of feminist critical literature is that the essence of art and biography and the correlation between them is conditional upon the question of gender. That Dickinson is a poet is intrinsic to her creativity. By disintegrating her individuality into two mutually restraining constituents, 'woman' and 'poet', conventional critical thought has typified two characters instead of one. More instances of such a rupture of identity takes place when her poetry exhibits traces of detachment from any significant evaluation as regards its relationship to the artist creating it. Feminist criticism endeavours to juxtapose these fragments together: 'woman' and 'poet'. As Suzanne Juhasz has indicated in her work entitled, 'Naked and Fiery Forms: Modern American Poetry by Women, A New Tradition',[10] critical literary analyses of Dickinson during both the nineteenth and twentieth centuries have predominantly made the differentiation between woman and poet. Actually, there has been a long-sustained emphasis on these elements being mutually restrictive. Studies as divergent in perspective as George Whicher's exemplary critique, *This was a Poet: A Critical Biography of Emily Dickinson*,[11] and John Cody's psychoanalytic account, *After Great Pain: The Inner Life of Emily Dickinson*, appear as noticeably corresponding inferences. While Whicher believes that the consummation of the woman lies in becoming the poet, Cody's conclusive observations are comparatively more overwhelming:

> It was Mrs. Dickinson's failure as a sufficiently loving and admirable developmental model that set in motion the series of psychological upheavals which were unmitigated misfortunes for Emily Dickinson, *the woman*. These maturational impasses consigned her to a life of sexual bewilderment, anxiety and frustration by impairing those processes of psychic growth which would have made the roles of wife and mother possible. With reference to Emily Dickinson the *artist*, one cannot speak of misfortunes at all. For, amazing as it may seem, Mrs. Dickinson's inadequacies, the sequence of internal conflicts to which they gave rise, and the final psychotic breakdown all conspired in a unique way to make of Emily Dickinson a great and prolific poet.[12]

Precisely what Cody enunciates is that, 'the violent disharmonies and unceasing restlessness of her inner life ... thus appear in her case to have contributed copiously to *the transformation of woman into poet*.'[13]

As the focus of feminist criticism is pivoted around Dickinson, its primary engagement is to examine and avow the obvious correlation between woman and poet. The predominant of such works, Elsa Green's 'Emily Dickinson was a Poetess', published in 1972, makes an effort to establish the argument with complete transparency:

> Unless Emily Dickinson's poems are approached as a woman's art based on female human experience, readers are free to avoid challenges to the clichés which have long served otherwise intelligent and thoughtful people as the truth about women.[14]

'Given her vocation', maintains Adrienne Rich, 'she was neither eccentric nor quaint; she was determined to survive, to use her powers, to practice necessary economies.'[15] When the two terms 'woman' and 'poet' are not regarded as interchangeably delimiting, there happens to be a thorough transposition in the approach in which both the occurrences in Dickinson's life and her works of poetry are understood. The significant dilemma no longer remains singular, since it begins to bear considerable import.

In her concluding paragraph, Rich unequivocally states the origin of these positions as they were:

> To say 'yes' to her powers was not simply a major act of nonconformity in the nineteenth century; even in our time it has been assumed that Emily Dickinson, not patriarchal society, was 'the problem'. The more we come to recognize the unwritten and written laws and taboos underpinning patriarchy, the less problematical, surely, will seem the methods she chose.[16]

From a feminist stance, neither was Dickinson's life a departure, nor was it an instance of circumvention and renunciation, but rather one of artistic manoeuvre and ingenuity that equipped her with the rare poetic acumen that she had. Rich affirms this in the following manner:

> It was a life deliberately organized on her terms. The terms she had been handed by society – Calvinist Protestantism, Romanticism, the nineteenth century corseting of women's bodies, choices, and sexuality – could spell insanity to a woman of genius.[17]

Rich identifies the potential vigour and significance of Dickinson's life and art. She considers her poetry as not only phenomenal, but essentially momentous to knowledge about the experiential world. Rich reads her works to be created by a 'mind engaged in a lifetime's musing on essential problems of language, identity, separation, relationship, the integrity of the self; a mind capable of describing psychological states more accurately than any poet except Shakespeare'.[18] She describes Dickinson's art as 'the poetry of extreme states, the poetry of danger', that 'can allow its readers to go further in our own awareness, take risks we might not have dared; it says, at least: "Someone has been here before."'[19]

In *Women Writers and Poetic Identity: Dorothy Wordsworth, Emily Brontë, and Emily Dickinson,*[20] Margaret Homans has examined Dickinson's language and its contribution in her formation as a woman artist. Homans's standpoint bases itself on both feminist and linguistic erudition of women poets in order to examine how the conventional association of women with the notion of 'otherness', both in the societal and in the cultural domains, is the pivotal hindrance they require to overcome in order to establish themselves as poets.

In her discourse of the patriarchal tradition, Homans describes how language demonstrates masculine suppositions:

> Language's operation is to identify otherness as self, to appropriate objects and transform them into subject. Adamic language, theoretically ideal because its words are synonymous with their meanings, is also the type of appropriative language, since Adam understood language to mean control over the beasts he named, and he named the woman as well.[21]

The quintessence of Dickinson's language was that she often deployed antithetical expressions to invert the traditional configurations of language in order to establish a poetic individuality through her percipience of femininity or the conventional idea of the 'other'.

Homans demonstrates how indistinguishable Dickinson is with Eve, who can understand and master other speech forms apart from those of Adam's, for instance, when Satan deceives, it facilitates her to comprehend the metaphorical use of language. 'She understands and makes use of a general dislocation between words and their referents.'[22] Dickinson undertakes to defy the hierarchical order in language, which forms the crux of male ascendency. Hence Homans corroborates, 'the desire to be at the center generates hierarchical thinking, but even the potentially neutral concept of opposition also turns into hierarchy, because it is impossible ever to be entirely disinterested and one element must be primary and the other secondary.'[23]

Homans encapsulates her thesis by way of what she avows in the following:

> This recognition of the fictionality of nature's traditional sexual identification is part of Dickinson's larger discovery about language's fictiveness. Her resistance to appropriating nature is one model for improving the status of the woman writer in relation to the tradition; another lies in her challenge to the assumption that opposition is necessary for language to have meaning. Her undoing of rhetorical dualism becomes a model for a revised pattern of relations between the sexes, in her recognition that the opposition of the sexes is as figurative as any other kind of opposition, not a literal necessity. The traditional determinisms that have maintained this opposition need no longer operate, just as the tradition of Mother Nature, once it is recognized as a tradition and therefore figurative, not actual, ceases to be confining. A tradition with masculine dominance may be at the root of dualistic language, and her feminine identity, particularly her sense of inheritance from Eve, may be the origin of her readiness to object to that structure of language. She disrupts traditional relations between the sexes by means of the kind of undoing of hierarchical language that she employs in poems about the idea of opposition itself. Dickinson brings to those poems in which the poet's identity is explicitly feminine her knowledge that her best power lies in the manipulation of language to reverse its ordinary meanings. She uses that linguistic power first to reverse the ordinary direction of power between a feminine self and a masculine other, and then, as in the poems where she undoes antithetical language, used it to discard the idea of dominance altogether.[24]

Homans puts forward these ideas through diligent, meticulous and conscientious reviews of Dickinson's poetry. Her effort is of momentous worth since it endorses the crucial feminist perspective, the inevitability of the correlation between woman and poet and the appreciation of the mastery that Dickinson accomplished by this correlation, and diversifies the relevance of these issues from the domain of biographical recollections into the probably more inspiring and more widely assorted panorama of poetry as a whole. Hence, as Homans indicates, dislocation, invalidation and transposition are fundamental to Dickinson's authority – the reconstruction of the patriarchal notions of art and language and the dichotomy in them – enabling her to formulate novel structures that are appropriate for her art. Her capacity to take control, to disconcert and to inverse is not an equivocation but a vigorous and a profound association with these very forms.

'"A Woman White": Emily Dickinson's Yarn of Pearl' is the concluding section of Gilbert and Gubar's pioneering study on nineteenth-century female writers. They are enthusiastic about the widely divergent dimensions of Dickinson's poetic impersonations. They are specifically engaged in deciphering the significance of the 'roles' that the poet plays. They affirm that Dickinson's 'posing' proved to be 'essential to her poetic self-achievement'.[25] The woman novelist creates a distinctive narrative intonation in which she is able to articulate her decisive self on the one hand, and on the other, she is able to enact the role of the subject herself. Hence, in Dickinson, they maintain, 'we see the culmination of this process, an almost complete absorption of the characters of the fiction into the persona of their author, so that this writer and her protagonist(s) become for all practical purposes one – one "supposed person" achieving the authority of self-creation by enacting many highly literary selves and lives'. 'For Dickinson, indeed', they deduce, 'art is not so much *poesis* – making – as it is *mimesis* – enactment, and this because she believes that even consciousness is not so much reflective as it is theatrical'.[26]

The initial Dickinsonian impersonation that Gilbert and Gubar contemplate considering all its intricacies is the 'Daisy', that is, the image of Dickinson as an infant. This context instantaneously precipitates the arguments about her approach towards the ideas of selfhood, art, love, men and the tradition of patriarchy and its constraints. They emphasize that her repudiation of her transformation into an adult woman, a kind of character carved by the society for her, was a trajectory enabling her to construct an authoritative self, but this perceptibly impinged upon her psychical and existential movement as well:

> Rather early in her life as artist, Dickinson must have half-consciously perceived that she could avoid the necessity of renouncing her art by renouncing, instead, that concept of womanliness which required self-abnegating renunciation. Or, to put it another way, she must have decided that to begin with she could try to solve the problem of being a woman by refusing to admit that she was a woman .... On the other hand ... the child mask (or pose or costume) eventually threatened to become a crippling self, a self that in the crisis of her gothic life fiction locked her into her father's house in the way that a little girl is confined to a nursery.[27]

The impersonation of the woman in white most embodies the intricacies of Dickinson's enterprise, with all its resilience and trepidations, and is her most enthralling stance in both life and art:

> That Dickinson's white dress implies not a single supposed person but a series of characters suggests, however, not just the artful complexity of her strategy for escaping Requirements but also the dangers implicit in that strategy. Impersonating simultaneously a "little maid" in white, a dead woman in white, and a ghost in white, Dickinson seems to have split herself into a series of incubae, haunting not just her father's house but her own mind .... The ambiguities and discontinuities implicit in her white dress became, therefore, as much signs of her own psychic fragmentation as of her society's multiple (and conflicting) demands upon women. As such, they objectified the enigma of the poet's true personality – for if she was both Daisy and Empress, child and ghost, who was she "really"?[28]

Eventually, the authors decipher an additional role of the spinner and the spider that they consider as unifying, and an imagery that not only befittingly epitomizes a corrosion in the patriarchal fallacy, but also typifies the necromancer, the sorceress, 'a crucial if "neglected" emblem of art, and of the artist as the most triumphant secret self'.[29] Analyzing the imagery contained in the spider poems of Dickinson, Gilbert and Gubar contemplate how 'all these poems seem to say that, as Dickinson defines it, female art must almost necessarily be secret art; mental pirouettes silently performed in the attic of Nobodaddy's house, the growth of an obscure underwater jewel, or, especially, a spider's unobtrusively woven yarn of pearl.'[30]

Gilbert and Gubar's book itself is much akin to the task of a spinner with the authors lending their thoughts to the images evident in Dickinson's poetry to substantiate the methods of perceiving the poet's anxiety and accomplishments. But, as Suzanne Juhasz points out: 'What they do not acknowledge is how these complexities and tensions are manifested in the poetry, itself, in its language and forms. They do not "read" poems; instead they search them for the images that, to use their own metaphor, "are loaded like so many pearls in these oysters, and use the garnered images to understand the biography".'[31] However, their idea of the dramatic component in Dickinson's life offers striking symbols both to understand its history and to make a significant appraisal of its imaginative evolution.

Karl Keller's study, *The Only Kangaroo among the Beauty: Emily Dickinson and America*,[32] is completely committed to Dickinson and is also the most enterprising work in Dickinson scholarship. He deciphered Dickinson's 'silences and slips' as being an essential element of her consciousness, apparently fragmentary and enervated, but actually unfathomably consummate:

> Saving a life like Emily Dickinson's from that hall of tortures called biography while saying something accurate and moving perhaps means leaving her silences and her slips alone – not the unknowns, but the white spaces where we have little or no ability to look with *our* eyes ...
>
> There is a life in her poems, but it is a life she fragments for us, and that is what one has – not pieces of a figure but sides, each one imagined or real as she understood it or as we do. The sides outline a figure without making it whole or fully satisfying. What went on in her life and mind moment by moment is unfathomable ....[33]

The book is not only edifying in its nature, but as well as a delight to read, especially tinged by his authoritative scholarship, his unassuming approach and his witticisms, thus unveiling Dickinson as immaculately human.

In ways both explicit and implicit, Keller takes up the matters concerning gender, feminism and Dickinson as a woman. He is certainly emphatic about the essential feminine element in her. He addresses the issue by saying, 'Her being a woman is an issue to us precisely because it was an issue to her.'[34] In the chapters that focus on the relationship between Dickinson and Anne Bradstreet, or the dynamic feminists of her time like Harriet Beecher Stowe, or the English women authors whom she significantly appreciated – the Bront's, George Eliot, Elizabeth Barrett Browning – Keller reveals how her studied consideration of her own gender enabled her to formulate a private world of her own by turning inward to her own self, a world that is profound, emancipating and domineering, providing her with the space she can 'play with':

> She appears to have sensed the inseparability of privacy and culture. For one thing, she had no institution – such as holy orders or prison or academia – to provide her with the detachment necessary for critical perspective, revaluation, or changes of course. She had to do it on her own. In that private space she had distance to see with and play with. This privacy was a natural advantage in a community that was culturally rich enough to be able to afford it. She was smart enough, too, to take advantage of it to build a world of her own.[35]

Keller, in the other chapters, describes her in contradistinction to male authors, for instance, Edwards, Hawthorne, Emerson and Whitman. He segregates her attributes that cannot be categorized as 'woman-like' but, at the same time, carry considerable implications of Dickinson as a woman writer, for example, her aversion to historicality of experience:

> For her, experience was never historical. Though she might often have wished it otherwise, Now preempted almost everything else.[36]

Another noticeable instance of femininity in her writing is the element of incongruity that she makes between privacy and irreproachable self-conceit:

> Her solipsism is not strong enough to impose a will on the world to make it yield, narcissistically, a pattern of herself.[37]

Again, her '*anti* philosophical' position is reflective of her quintessential womanliness:

> ... Emily Dickinson was the first really *anti*philosophical poet in American literature. A poetry of experience categorically denies the possibility of a poetry of comment, of ratiocination; a poetry of sensation goes even further in closing off its universe to the *merely* felt, the profoundly thought. If Emily Dickinson's epigrams *seem* profound, it is their seeming so that their unit is, like that of her poems, viscerally wrung from the strictures of daily experience .... Swinging thus between improvisation and aphorism, between her confused experience and the hopefully sure universal, between metaphor and idea, she proceeds with the illusion that the making of meaning gives life quality.[38]

Thus, if quality is assured by the emergence of meaning, we are in a position to have recourse to the notion that it is only in the complex subtleties and nuances of language that meaning is embedded. The eloquence with which Dickinson expresses her profound experience of life reveals myriad significations and the veracity contained in them proves to be ingenuous. Certainly, in the midst of such profundity, she remains baffled and her deployment of aphorisms lends substantial corroboration to her 'confused experience'. Her epigrammatic language touches such dizzying heights of realization of the experiential world that it remains virtually enigmatic and hence, esoteric.

Keller also puts forward amidst his biographical and metaphorical explorations of gender, the idea of power. For him, Dickinson's power originates from her arrogation of the traditional and prevalent formations of social beliefs and institutions to construct a world and an identity of her own. Demonstrating the correlation between such power and the structures of the contemporary social world, he illustrates with the following interpretation of 'suttee', a custom that feminist critics like Mary Daly[39] have considered as a remorseless manifestation of female defacement carried out by patriarchy:

> *Suortù*: a woman defying her fate. Was that Emily Dickinson? I think she was really a headier version of that .... A woman defying her fate is what a man would expect of a woman. A woman accepting her fate to defy means accepting one's nature, one's humanity, one's gender, one's difference, one's ability, oneself.[40]

Hence, the acts of defying and reconstructing contribute to the emergence of this power. An examination of the jargon that feminist critics have used shall facilitate us in comprehending the nature of power that Dickinson cultivated. Joanne Feit Diehl, in his essay, '"Ransom in a Voice": Language as Defense in Dickinson's Poetry' explains thus:

> Adopting qualities associated with the Christian deity and transforming these into a linguistic process that she describes as both more human and equable than the Christian, Dickinson creates an alternative power potentially subversive of any external authority based upon the sovereignty of a male-identified divinity or predicated upon the supremacy of those within the religious fold.[41]

If we are to entirely fathom Dickinson's 'alternative power' that is 'potentially subversive', we have to recognize not only her accomplishments, but also the manner in which she accomplished. Sandra Gilbert, enunciating in her essay on the 'curiously theatrical language evoked by Dickinson's odd combinations of speech and silence, frankness and mystery', deduces:

> For if the mysteries of this poet's life are often riddles of absence or silence, then the mysteries of her art are marvels of transformation, 'conversions of the mind'(# 593)[42] in which we see a great performer turning defeat into triumph like a magician changing water into wine.[43]

Again, Adalaide Morris remarks on the imagery of her love poems in the following manner:

> The linked imagery of intensity, explosiveness, suppression, and mutilation suggests the extravagance of Dickinson's commitments.[44]

Expressions like 'extravagance', 'explosiveness' and those pertaining to the 'theatrical' bear testimony to the enormity of Dickinson's formidable art. Her creative acumen unveils itself through a diction which is emblematic of that power that allures us towards her poetry. Her presumptuous audacity, her witticisms, her aggression and her exuberance make her not merely delightful, but regal and sumptuous. In spite of the fact that she did not publish, the 'extravagance' of her verse paves the path for us to make an entry into her world, though perhaps seldom intended by her, since it calls for a close observation and a closer appreciation. The aptitude of reading Emily Dickinson in concordance with what she describes herself to be, certainly demands a measure of ingenuity. She is stupendously capacious and equally enigmatic, bountiful and enriching.

Suzanne Juhasz talks about words that 'occur and reoccur: *critique*, *strategy*, *subversion*, *appropriation*, *deviation*, *renunciation*, *transformation*, *control*, *possibility*'.[45] She expatiates on the uniqueness of the idea of power that Dickinson developed:

> These new essays, with their overlapping themes, show Dickinson first understanding her situation (*critique*) and then enacting in various ways (*strategy*) her attempts at solution. *Subversion*, *appropriation*, *deviation* are all kinds of *sabotage*, working upon the system, working within the system, using its own elements to turn them on purpose to her purposes. *Renunciation* is really a particular form of appropriation upon which Dickinson relied. The giving up of something valued may look like self-denial and is a firmly rooted patriarchal expectation for women (suttee being one of its extremest forms), but as a way of saying 'no' it can also be, and was for Dickinson, an act of autonomy. It cleared a space. A space wherein *transformation* might occur. But a space within the patriarchy. For transformation is the kind of magic that turns what is there at hand into something else. Something suddenly new, a creation. Transformation is a more practical, and more political, kind of magic than, say, fantasy. It is Dickinson's stock in trade.

Transformation leads both to *control* and to *possibility.* Control, an enactment of power, requires the presence of an other, be it society, nature, person, or aspect of self. Control reminds us of the existing presence of the world. *Possibility* is beyond. It is the direction in which Dickinson always heads, and it is a space she sometimes creates for herself, after a transformation has taken place. Control and possibility are aspects of her power.[46]

Juhasz's comment brings us not merely to infer, but believe that Dickinson critiqued and questioned the most basic premises and assumptions of female authorship by way of deploying language in such a way as to unsettle all notions of writing and creation being an exclusively male intellectual exercise. There remains a vista of possibility in their works, whereby they have been able to transform their anxiety of such secluded art into a subversive genre that was able to give expression to their life and experience. They, in ways both direct and covert, renounced their socially constructed roles and triumphed in carving out a paradigm shift in the way in which female authorship was estimated and received in the nineteenth century. Their poetry leaves for the subsequent generation of critics of women's writing such a rich plethora of significations on women's experiences both in life and in art, that much of them perhaps have remained even hitherto unexplored.

References

1. Adrienne Rich, 'When We Dead Awaken', in *On Lies, Secrets, and Silence: Selected Prose 1966-1978* (New York: W. W. Norton & Company Ltd., 1995), p. 39, in Jan Montefiore, *Feminism and Poetry: Language, Experience, Identity in Women's Writing* (London: Pandora Press, Routledge & Kegan Paul Ltd., 1987), p. 26.
2. Sandra M. Gilbert and Susan Gubar, *The Madwoman in the Attic: The Woman Writer and the Nineteenth Century Literary Imagination* (New Haven and London: Yale University Press, 1979), pp. 38-39.
3. Mary Jacobus, 'Review of The Madwoman in the Attic', in *Signs,* Vol. 6, no. 3 (Chicago: The University of Chicago Press, Spring 1981), pp. 517-18.

4. Montefiore, *Feminism and Poetry: Language, Experience, Identity in Women's Writing*, p. 29.
5. Gilbert and Gubar, *The Madwoman in the Attic*, p. 113.
6. *Ibid.*, p. 71.
7. Matthew Arnold's phrase for Charlotte Bronte's novel Villette, quoted in *The Madwoman in the Attic*, p. 337.
8. Gilbert and Gubar put forward most of these suggestions in The Madwoman in the Attic, pp. 545-49.
9. Hutton, R. H., 'Novels by the Authoress of John Halifax', North British Review 29, 1858, p. 467.
10. Suzanne Juhasz, *Naked and Fiery Forms: Modern American Poetry by Women*, A New Tradition (New York: Harper and Row, 1976), pp. 7-32.
11. George Whicher, *This was a Poet: A Critical Biography of Emily Dickinson* (Ann Arbor: The University of Michigan Press, 1938).
12. John Cody, *After Great Pain: The Inner Life of Emily Dickinson* (Cambridge, Massachusetts: Harvard University Press, 1971), p. 404.
13. *Ibid.*, p. 492.
14. Elsa Green, 'Emily Dickinson was a Poetess', in *College English 34*, October 1972, pp. 63-70.
15. Adrienne Rich, '"Vesuvius at Home": The Power of Emily Dickinson', in eds. Sandra M. Gilbert and Susan Gubar, *Shakespeare's Sisters: Feminist Essays on Women Poets* (Bloomington and London: Indiana University Press, 1979), p. 101.
16. *Ibid.*, p. 121.
17. *Ibid.*, p. 102.
18. *Ibid.*, p. 107.
19. *Ibid.*, p. 107.
20. Margaret Homans, *Women Writers and Poetic Identity: Dorothy Wordsworth, Emily Brontë, and Emily Dickinson* (Princeton, N. J.: Princeton University Press, 1980).
21. *Ibid.*, p. 37.
22. *Ibid.*, p. 193.
23. *Ibid.*, p. 36.

24. Margaret Homans, *Women Writers and Poetic Identity: Dorothy Wordsworth, Emily Brontë, and Emily Dickinson* (Princeton, N. J.: Princeton University Press, 1980), p. 201.
25. Gilbert and Gubar, *The Madwoman in the Attic*, p. 584.
26. *Ibid.*, p. 586.
27. *Ibid.*, pp. 590-91.
28. *Ibid.*, pp. 621-22.
29. *Ibid.*, p. 633.
30. *Ibid.*, p. 634.
31. Suzanne Juhasz ed., 'Introduction', in *Feminist Critics Read Emily Dickinson* (Bloomington: Indiana University Press, 1983), p. 15.
32. Karl Keller, *The Only Kangaroo among the Beauty: Emily Dickinson and America* (Baltimore and London: John Hopkins University Press, 1979).
33. *Ibid.*, p. 2.
34. *Ibid.*, p. 35.
35. *Ibid.*, p. 241.
36. *Ibid.*, p. 106.
37. *Ibid.*, p. 118.
38. *Ibid.*, pp. 180-81.
39. Mary Daly, *Beyond God the Father* (Boston: Beacon Press, 1973); *Gyn-Ecology: The Metaethics of Radical Feminism* (Boston: Beacon Press, 1990).
40. Karl Keller, 'Notes on Sleeping with Emily Dickinson', in ed. Suzanne Juhasz, Feminist Critics Read Emily Dickinson, p. 68.
41. Joanne Feit Diehl, '"Ransom in a Voice": Language as Defense in Dickinson's Poetry', in ed. Suzanne Juhasz, *Feminist Critics Read Emily Dickinson*, p. 157.
42. Emily Dickinson, Poem 593. All Emily-Dickinson Poems from 495 to 1775 are taken from the following e-Source: *http://archive.csustan.edu/english/reuben/pal/chap4/dickinson.html* (Thomas H. Johnson ed. *Complete Poems* [Boston: Little, Brown & Co., 1960], as a part of PAL: Perspectives in American Literature – A Research and Reference Guide, An Ongoing Online Project, Paul P. Reuben [copyright]).

43. Sandra M. Gilbert, "The Wayward Nun beneath the Hill": Emily Dickinson and the Mysteries of Womanhood', in ed. Suzanne Juhasz, *Feminist Critics Read Emily Dickinson*, p. 27.

44. Adalaide Morris, "The Love of Thee – A Prism Be": Men and Women in the Love Poems of Emily Dickinson', in ed. Suzanne Juhasz, *Feminist Critics Read Emily Dickinson*, p. 101.

45. Suzanne Juhasz ed., 'Introduction', in *Feminist Critics Read Emily Dickinson*, p. 18.

46. *Ibid.*, pp. 18-19.

Bibliography

(A) Primary Sources

(i) Print

Coleridge, S.T., Introductory note to his 'Hymn Before Sun-rise, In the Vale of Chamouni', in the *Morning Post*, September 11, 1802.

– – , *Poetical Works*, ed. Ernest Hartley Coleridge, London: Oxford University Press, 1967.

Dickinson, Emily, *The Letters of Emily Dickinson*, 3 vols., eds. Thomas H. Johnson and Theodora Ward, Cambridge, Massachusetts: Harvard University Press, 1958.

– –, *Emily Dickinson: Selected Letters*, ed. Thomas H. Johnson, Cambridge, Massachusetts: Harvard University Press, 1958.

Elizabeth Barrett Browning, *The Letters of Elizabeth Barrett Browning*, 2 vols. ed. Frederic G. Kenyon (New York: Macmillan, 1897), Vol. I, pp. 231-2.

Hopkins, Gerard Manley, and Richard Watson Dixon, *The Correspondence of Gerard Manley Hopkins and Richard Watson Dixon*, ed. C.C. Abbott, London: Oxford University Press, 1935.

Nightingale, Florence, *Cassandra*, New York: Westbury, 1979.

Whitman, Walt, *The Complete Poems*, New York: Penguin, 1975.

Wordsworth, William, 'Tintern Abbey', in *The Complete Poetical Works*, introd. John Morley, London: Macmillan, 1888.

– – , *The Prelude: A Parallel Text*, ed. J. C. Maxwell, Harmondsworth: Penguin, 1975.

(ii) Electronic Sources

Dickinson, Emily, *The Poems of Emily Dickinson*, 3 vols. ed. Thomas H. Johnson (Cambridge, Massachusetts: Harvard University Press, 1955], Vol. 1 [Poems

1-494]). Source: https://ia700301.us.archive.org/2/items/poemsofemilydick030097mbp/poemsofemilydick030097mbp.pdf

Dickinson, Emily, *Complete Poems* ed. Thomas H. Johnson [Boston: Little, Brown & Co., 1960], as a part of PAL: Perspectives in American Literature – A Research and Reference Guide, An Ongoing Online Project, Paul P. Reuben [copyright]. Source: http://archive.csustan.edu/english/reuben/pal/chap4/dickinson.html

Dickinson, Emily, *The Letters of (Le lettere di) Emily Dickinson.* Source: http://www.emilydickinson.it/letters.html

(B) Secondary Sources

(i) Books

Abel, Elizabeth, ed., *Writing and Sexual Difference*, Chicago: Chicago University Press, 1982.

Abel, Elizabeth, and Emily K. Abel eds., *The Signs Reader: Women, Gender and Scholarship*, Chicago: Chicago University Press, 1983.

Anderson, Charles R., *Emily Dickinson's Poetry: A Stairway of Surprise*, New York: Holt, Rinehart and Winston, 1960.

Armstrong, Isobel, *Victorian Scrutinies: Reviews of Poetry, 1830-1870*, London: The Athlone Press, 1972.

– – , *Language as Living Form in Nineteenth-Century Poetry*, Brighton: Harvester Press, 1982.

Armstrong, Isobel and Joseph Bristow with Cath Sharrock eds., *Nineteenth-Century Women Poets: An Oxford Anthology*, Oxford: Clarendon Press, 1996.

Auerbach, Nina, *Woman and the Demon: The Life of a Victorian Myth*, Cambridge, Massachusetts: Harvard University Press, 1982.

Bald, Marjorie Amelia, *Women Writers of the Nineteenth Century*, Cambridge: Cambridge University Press, 1923.

Beauvoir, Simone de, *The Second Sex*, New York: Alfred A. Knopf Inc., 1952.

Bennett, Paula, *'My Life, a Loaded Gun': Female Creativity and Feminist Poetics*, Boston: Beacon Press, 1986.

– –, ed., *Nineteenth-Century American Women Poets: An Anthology*, Malden, Massachusetts: Blackwell Publishing, 1998.

Berger, John, *Ways of Seeing*, Penguin Books: British Broadcasting Corporation, 1977.

Blake, Caesar Robert, and Carlton Frank Wells eds., *The Recognition of Emily Dickinson: Selected Criticism since 1890*, Ann Arbor: The University of Michigan Press, 1968.

Blank, G. Kim, and Louis, Margot K., *Influence and Resistance in Nineteenth-Century English Poetry*, London: Macmillan, 1993.

Bloom, Harold, *The Anxiety of Influence: A Theory of Poetry*, New York and Oxford: Oxford University Press, 1973.

– –, *A Map of Misreading*, Oxford: Oxford University Press, 1975.

Bowra, C. M., *The Romantic Imagination*, New York: Oxford University Press, 1961.

Brewer, Mary, *Exclusions in Feminist Thought: Challenging the Boundaries of Womanhood*, Brighton: Sussex Academic Press, 2002.

Bristow, Joseph, ed., *The Victorian Poet: Poetics and Persona*, London: Croom Helm, 1987.

– – , ed., *The Cambridge Companion to Victorian Poetry*, Cambridge: Cambridge University Press, 2000.

Budick, E. Miller, *Emily Dickinson and the Life of Language: A Study in Symbolist Poetics*, Baton Rouge: Louisiana State University Press, 1985.

Caine, Barbara, *Victorian Feminists*, Oxford: Oxford University Press, 1992.

Chevigny, Bell Gale, *The Woman and the Myth: Margaret Fuller's Life and Writings*, Boston: Northeastern University Press, 1994.

Clark, G. Kitson, *The Making of Victorian England*, London: Methuen, 1977.

Cody, John, *After Great Pain: The Inner Life of Emily Dickinson*, Cambridge, Massachusetts: Harvard University Press, 1971.

Cosslett, Tess, ed., *Victorian Women Poets*, London: Longmans, 1997.

Cunliffe, John, *Leaders of the Victorian Revolution*, New York: D. Appleton-Century Co., 1934.

Cushman, Stephen, *Fictions of Form in American Poetry*, Princeton, N.J.: Princeton University Press, 1993.

Daly, Mary, *Beyond God the Father*, Boston: Beacon Press, 1973.

– –, *Gyn-Ecology: The Metaethics of Radical Feminism*, Boston: Beacon Press, 1990.

Delamont, Sara, and Duffin Lorna, *The Nineteenth-Century Woman: Her Cultural and Physical World*, London: Croom Helm, 1978.

Diehl, Joanne Feit, *Dickinson and the Romantic Imagination*, Princeton, N. J.: Princeton University Press, 1981.

Eberle, Roxanne, *Chastity and Transgression in Women's Writing, 1792-1897*, Basingstoke, Hampshire: Palgrave Macmillan, 2002.

Eberwein, Jane Donahue, *Dickinson: Strategies of Limitation*, Amherst: The University of Massachusetts Press, 1985.

Ellis, Sarah, *The Mothers of England*, in *The Prose Works*, 2 vols., New York: Langley, 1844.

Emerson, Ralph Waldo, *The Journals and Miscellaneous Notebooks of Ralph Waldo Emerson*, Vol. VIII, 1841-3, eds. William Gilman and J.E. Parsons, Cambridge: Massachusetts, Harvard University Press, 1978.

Faderman, Lilian, *Surpassing the Love of Men: Romantic Friendship and Love between Women from the Renaissance to the Present*, London: Routledge & Kegan Paul, 1985.

Faverty, Frederic Everett, ed., *The Victorian Poets: A Guide to Research*, Second Edition, Cambridge, Massachusetts: Harvard University Press, 1968.

Ferlazzo, Paul, ed., *Critical Essays on Emily Dickinson*, Boston: G.K. Hall, 1984.

Freud, Sigmund, *The Interpretation of Dreams,* trans. A. A. Brill, New York: Macmillan, 1913; Published online by Bartleby.com in August 2010.

Gelpi, Albert J., *Emily Dickinson: The Mind of the Poet*, Cambridge, Massachusetts: Harvard University Press, 1965.

––, *The Tenth Muse: The Psyche of the American Poet*, Cambridge, Massachusetts: Harvard University Press, 1975.

Gelpi, Barbara Charlesworth, and Albert J. Gelpi eds., *Adrienne Rich's Poetry*, New York: Norton, 1975.

Gilbert, Sandra M., and Susan Gubar, *The Madwoman in the Attic: The Woman Writer and the Nineteenth Century Literary Imagination*, New Haven and London: Yale University Press, 1979.

, eds., *Shakespeare's Sisters. Feminist Essays on Women Poets*, Bloomington: Indiana University Press, 1979.

Gill, Stephen, ed., *William Wordsworth*, Oxford: Oxford University Press, 1984.

Gorham, Deborah, *The Victorian Girl and the Feminine Ideal*, London: Croom Helm, 1982.

Grabher, Gudrun, Roland Hagenbuchlë and Cristanne Miller eds., *The Emily Dickinson Handbook*, Amherst: University of Massachusetts Press, 1998.

Griffith, Clark, *The Long Shadow: Emily Dickinson's Tragic Poetry*, Princeton, N.J.: Princeton University Press, 1964.

Hellerstein, Erna Olafson, Leslie Parker Hume and Karen M. Offen eds., *Victorian Women: A Documentary Account of Women's Lives in Nineteenth-Century England, France and the United States*, Brighton, England: Harvester Press, 1981.

Helsinger, Elizabeth K., Robin Lauterbach Sheets and Wiliam Veeder, *The Woman Question: Society and Literature in Britain and America, 1837-1883*, Manchester: Manchester University Press, 1983.

Hilles, Frederick W., and Harold Bloom eds., *From Sensibility to Romanticism*, New York: Oxford University Press, 1965.

Holloway, John, *Proud Knowledge: Poetry, Insight and the Self, 1620-1920*, London: Routledge & Kegan Paul, 1977.

Homans, Margaret, *Women Writers and Poetic Identity: Dorothy Wordsworth, Emily Brontë, and Emily Dickinson*, Princeton, N.J.: Princeton University Press, 1980.

– –, *Bearing the Word: Language and Female Experience in Nineteenth-Century Women's Writing*, Chicago: Chicago University Press, 1986.

Hoy, Pat C., Esther H. Schor and Robert Di Yanni eds., *Women's Voices: Visions and Perspectives*, New York: McGraw-Hill, 1990.

Jacobus, Mary, ed., *Women Writing and Writing about Women*, London: Croom Helm, in association with Oxford University Women's Studies Committee, 1979.

– –, *Reading Woman: Essays in Feminist Criticism*, London: Methuen, 1986.

Jenkins, Ruth, *Reclaiming Myths of Power: Women Writers and the Victorian Spiritual Crisis*, Lewisburg: Bucknell University Press, 1995.

Johnson, Greg, *Emily Dickinson: Perception and the Poet's Quest*, Alabama: Alabama University Press, 1985.

Juhasz, Suzanne, *Naked and Fiery Forms: Modern American Poetry by Women, A New Tradition*, New York: Harper and Row, 1976.

– –, *The Undiscovered Continent: Emily Dickinson and the Space of the Mind*, Bloomington: Indiana University Press, 1983.

– –, ed., *Feminist Critics Read Emily Dickinson*, Bloomington: Indiana University Press, 1983.

Keller, Karl, *The Only Kangaroo among the Beauty: Emily Dickinson and America*, Baltimore and London: John Hopkins University Press, 1979.

Kenner, Hugh, *The Pound Era*, Berkeley and Los Angeles: University of California Press, 1971.

Keohane, Nannerl O., Michelle Z. Rosaldo and Barbara Charlesworth Gelpi eds., *Feminist Theory: A Critique of Ideology*, Brighton: Harvester Press, 1982.

Kher, Inder Nath, *The Landscape of Absence: Emily Dickinson's Poetry*, New Haven: Yale University Press, 1974.

Lacan, Jacques, *The Language of the Self: The Function of Language in Psychoanalysis*, Baltimore: The Johns Hopkins University Press, 1968.

Lease, Benjamin, *Emily Dickinson's Readings of Men and Books*, New York: St. Martin's Press, 1990.

Leighton, Angela, *Victorian Women Poets: Writing against the Heart*, Hemel Hempstead: Harvester Wheatsheaf, 1992.

– –, ed., *Victorian Women Poets: A Critical Reader*, Oxford: Blackwell Publishing, 1996.

Lewis, Magda Gere, *Without a Word: Teaching Beyond Women's Silence*, New York: Routledge, 1993.

Lindberg-Seyersted, Brita, *The Voice of the Poet: Aspects of Style in the Poetry of Emily Dickinson*, Cambridge: Harvard University Press, 1968.

Littledale, R. W., *The Religious Education of Women*, London: Henry S. King & Co., 1874.

Loades, Ann, *Feminist Theology: Voices from the Past*, Cambridge: Polity Press, 2001.

Loeffelholz, Mary, *Dickinson and the Boundaries of Feminist Theory*, Illinois: The University of Illinois Press, 1991.

Marsh, Jan, *Pre-Raphaelite Sisterhood*, London: Quartet Books, 1985.

Martin, Wendy, *Cambridge Companion to Emily Dickinson*, Cambridge: Cambridge University Press, 2002.

McGlen, Nancy E., and Karen O' Connor, *Women's Rights: The Struggle for Equality in the Nineteenth and Twentieth Centuries*, New York: Praeger, 1983.

Mellor, Anne, *Romanticism and Gender*, New York: Routledge, 1993.

Mendus, Susan, and Jane Rendall eds., *Sexuality and Subordination: Interdisciplinary Studies of Gender in the Nineteenth Century*, London: Routledge, 1989.

Miller, Ruth, *The Poetry of Emily Dickinson*, Middletown, C.T.: Wesleyan University Press, 1968.

Moi, Toril, *Sexual/Textual Politics: Feminist Literary Theory*, London: Routledge, 1985.

Montefiore, Jan, *Feminism and Poetry: Language, Experience, Identity in Women's Writing*, London: Pandora Press, Routledge & Kegan Paul Ltd., 1987.

Oberhaus, Dorothy H., *Emily Dickinson's Fascicles: Method and Meaning*, University Park: The Pennsylvania State University Press, 1995.

Phillips, Elizabeth, *Emily Dickinson: Personae and Performance*, University Park and London: The Pennsylvania State University Press, 1988.

Pollak, Vivian, *Dickinson: The Anxiety of Gender*, Ithaca and London: Cornell University Press, 1984.

Pollitt, Josephine, *Emily Dickinson: The Human Background of her Poetry*, New York: Cooper Square Publishers, 1970.

Porter, David, *Dickinson: The Modern Idiom*, Cambridge, Massachusetts: Harvard University Press, 1981.

Rank, Otto, *Art and Artist: Creative Urge and Personality Development* [1932], trans. Charles Francis Atkinson, New York: Alfred A. Knopf Inc., 1943.

Rees, Barbara, *The Victorian Lady*, London: Gordon & Cremonesi Publishers, 1977.

Roe, Sue, ed., *Women Reading Women's Writing*, Brighton: Harvester Press, 1987.

Sage, Lorna, *The Cambridge Guide to Women's Writing in English*, Cambridge: Cambridge University Press, 1999.

Sanders, Mike, ed. & introd., *Women and Radicalism in the Nineteenth Century*, London: Routledge, 2001.

Sewall, Richard B., *The Life of Emily Dickinson*, London: Faber & Faber, 1976.

– –, ed., *Emily Dickinson: A Collection of Critical Essays*, Englewood Cliffs, N.J.: Prentice Hall, 1963.

Slinn, E. Warwick, *The Discourse of Self in Victorian Poetry*, Charlottesville: University of Virginia Press, 1991.

Stott, Rebecca, *The Fabrication of the Late Victorian Femme Fatale: The Kiss of Death*, Basingstoke: Macmillan, 1992.

Thackrey, Donald E., *Emily Dickinson's Approach to Poetry*, Brooklyn: Haskell House Publishers Ltd., 1976.

Thompson, Nicole Diane, ed., *Victorian Women Writers and the Woman Question*, Cambridge: Cambridge University Press, 1999.

Thomson, Alexander Hamilton, *Cambridge History of English Literature*, New York: Macmillan, 1917, Vol. 13, Part 2.

Unger, Leonard, editor-in-chief, *American Writers: A Collection of Literary Biographies*, University of Minnesota: Charles Scribner's Sons, 1974.

Vicinus, Martha, *A Widening Sphere: Changing Roles of Victorian Women*, London: Methuen, 1980.

Waugh, Arthur, *Reticence in Literature*, London: J.G. Wilson, 1915.

Weisbuch, Robert, *Emily Dickinson's Poetry*, Chicago: Chicago University Press, 1975.

Whicher, George, *This was a Poet: A Critical Biography of Emily Dickinson*, Ann Arbor: The University of Michigan Press, 1938.

Wilcox, Helen, Keith McWatters, Ann Thompson and Linda R. Williams eds., *The Body and the Text: Hélène Cixous, Reading and Teaching*, Hemel Hempstead: Harvester Wheatsheaf, 1990.

Woolf, Virginia, *The Common Reader: Second Series*, London: Hogarth Press, 1953.

(ii) Articles and Book Chapters

Derrida, Jacques, 'La Question du style', in *Nietzsche aujourd'hui?*, Paris: Centre Culturel de Cerisy-La-Salle, 1973, I, pp. 235-87; also published in a four-language edition, translated into English as *Spurs: Nietzsche's Styles*, trans. Barbara Harlow, Venice: Corbo e Fiore, 1976.

– –, trans. Willis Domingo, James Hulbert, Moshe Ron, and Marie-Rose Logan, 'The Purveyor of Truth', in *Graphesis: Perspectives in Literature and Philosophy, Yale French Studies* 52, New Haven, Conn.: Yale University Press, 1975 (pp. 31-113), translated from 'Le Facteur de la verite', in *Poetique* 21, 1975, pp. 96-147.

Green, Elsa, 'Emily Dickinson was a Poetess', in *College English* 34, October 1972, pp. 63-70.

Hutton, R. H., 'Novels by the Authoress of *John Halifax*', *North British Review* 29, 1858, pp. 466-81.

Jacobus, Mary, 'Review of *The Madwoman in the Attic*', in *Signs*, Vol. 6, no. 3, Chicago: The University of Chicago Press, Spring 1981, pp. 517-23.

Mermin, Dorothy, 'The Damsel, the Knight, and the Victorian Woman Poet', in *Critical Enquiry*, 13, 1986, pp. 64-80.

Waslin, Sue, 'The Significance of Mary Daly's Thought for Feminist Theology', in Alison E. Jasper and Alastair Hunter eds. *Talking it Over: Perspectives on Women and Religion, 1993-1995*, Glasgow: Trinity St. Mungo Press, 1996, pp. 169-93.

Wasserman, Earl R., 'The English Romantics: The Grounds of Knowledge', in R. F. Gleckner and G.E. Enscoe eds. *Romanticism: Points of View*, 2nd edition, Detroit: Wayne State University Press, 1979, pp. 331-46.

'Women's Exile: Interview with Luce Irigaray' in *Ideology and Consciousness* 1, Paris: Minuit, 1977, pp. 62-76.

(iii) Electronic Sources

Burke, Edmund, *A Philosophical Inquiry into the Origin of Our Ideas of the Sublime and Beautiful*, New York: Bartleby.com, 2001. Source: www.bartleby.com/24/2/

More, Paul Elmer, *Toronto Shelburne Essays*, Third Series, G. P. Putnam's Sons, New York and London: Gbe Knickerbocker, 1907.

Source: http://www.archive.org/stream/shelburneessayss03moreuoft/shelburneessayss03moreuoft_djvu.txt

White, Edmund, Review of Hermione Lee's *Edith Wharton*, in *The New York Review of Books*, quoted by Steve Donoghue in 'Mount Wharton'. Source: http://www.openlettersmonthly.com/mount-wharton

Index